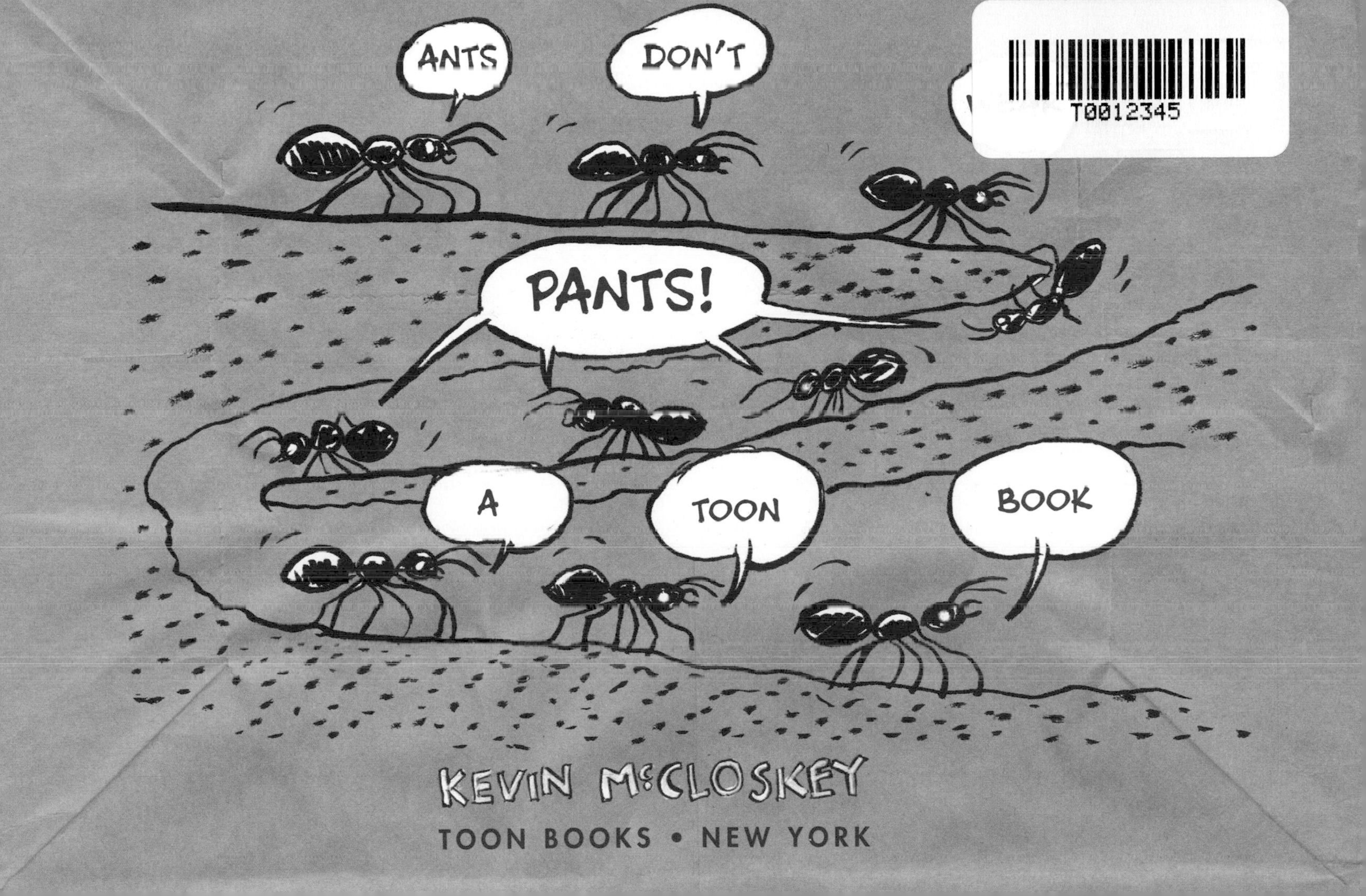
ANTS
DON'T
PANTS!
A
TOON
BOOK

KEVIN McCLOSKEY

TOON BOOKS • NEW YORK

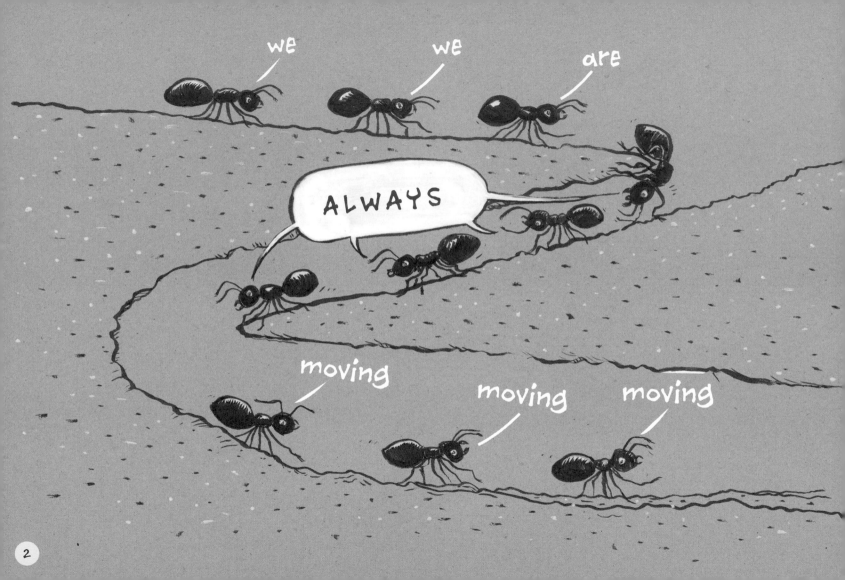

WHEN YOU CAN'T STOP MOVING,
WE SAY YOU HAVE "ANTS IN YOUR PANTS."

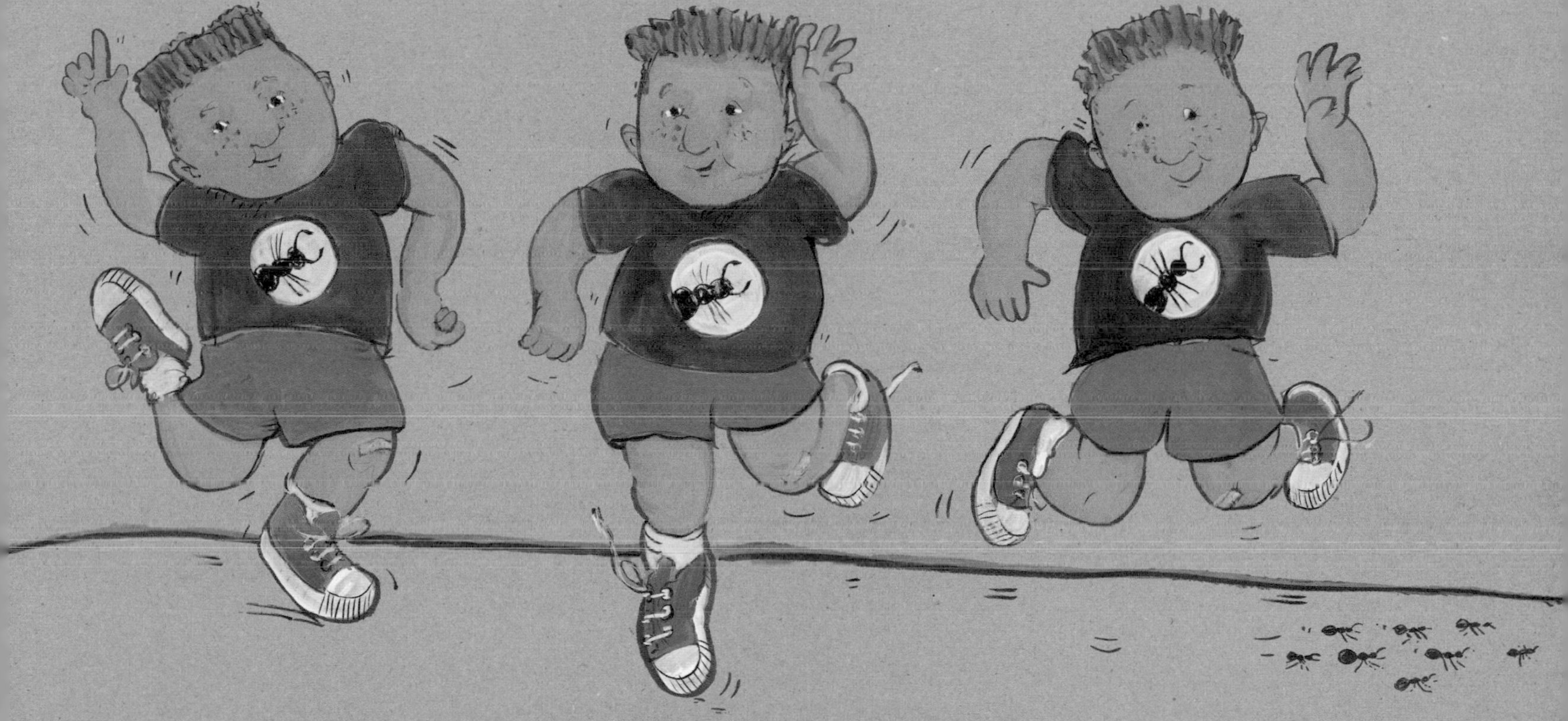

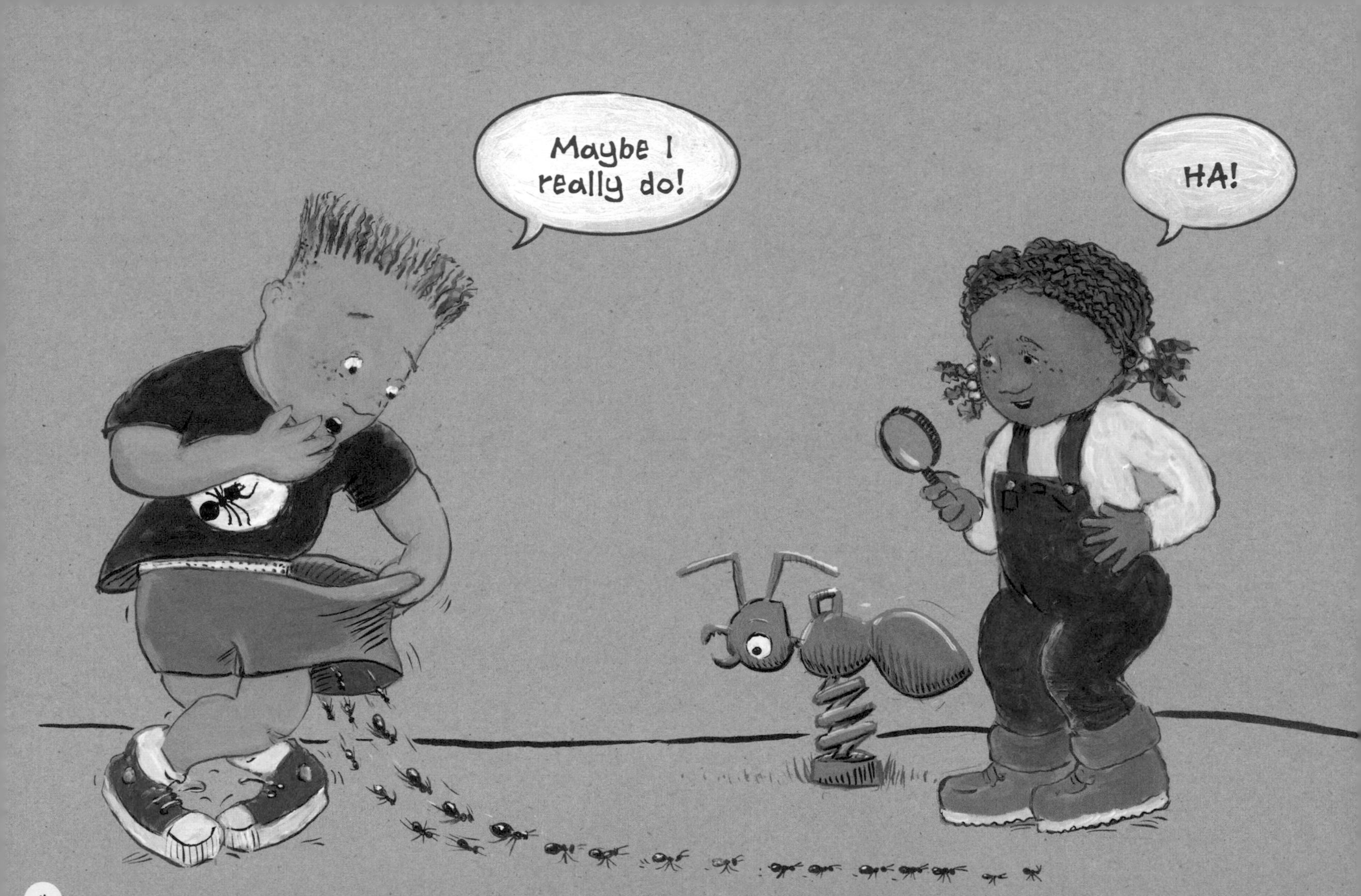
Maybe I really do!
HA!

ANTS ARE ALL AROUND US. LOOK AND YOU WILL FIND ANTHILLS.

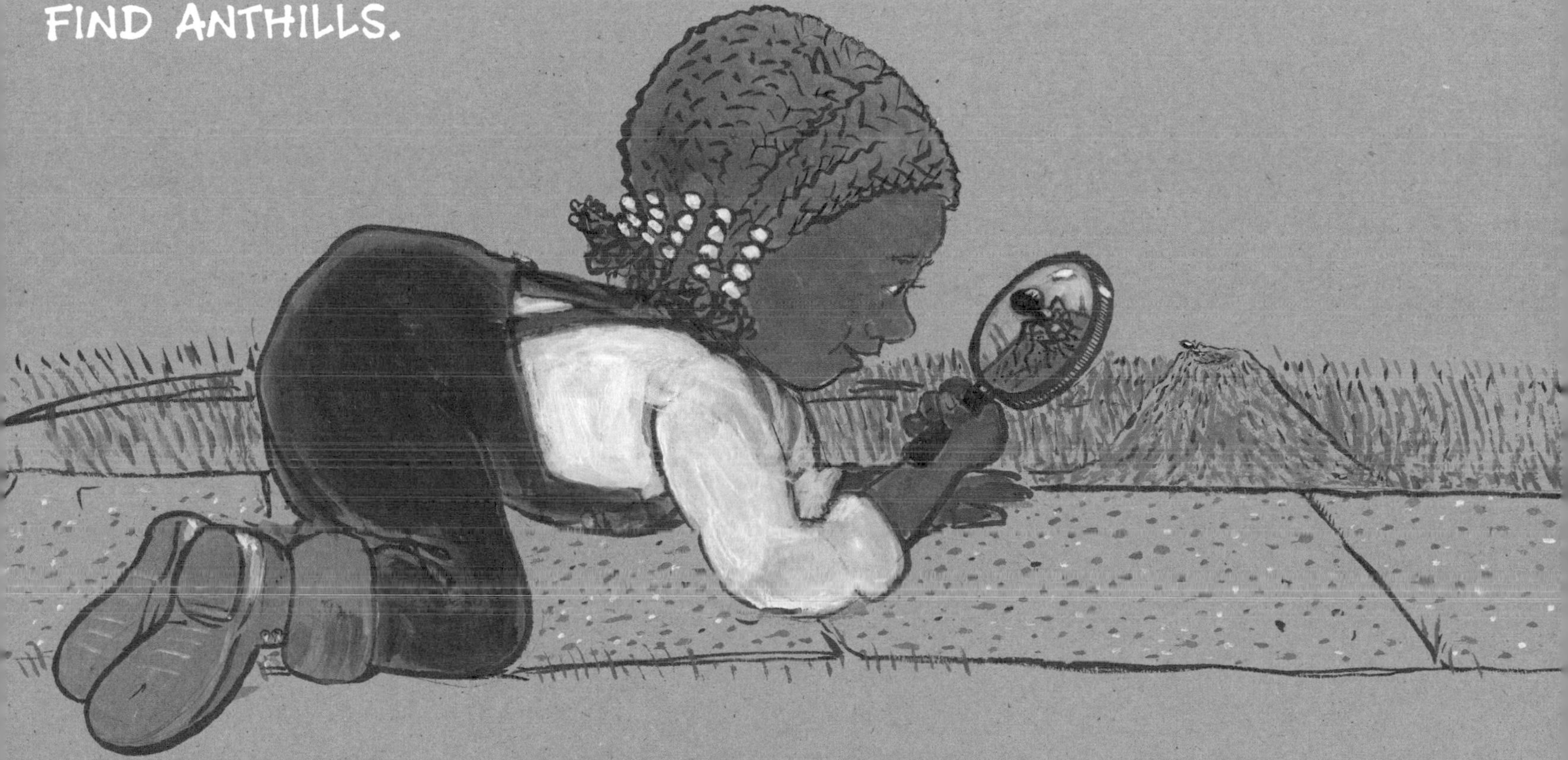

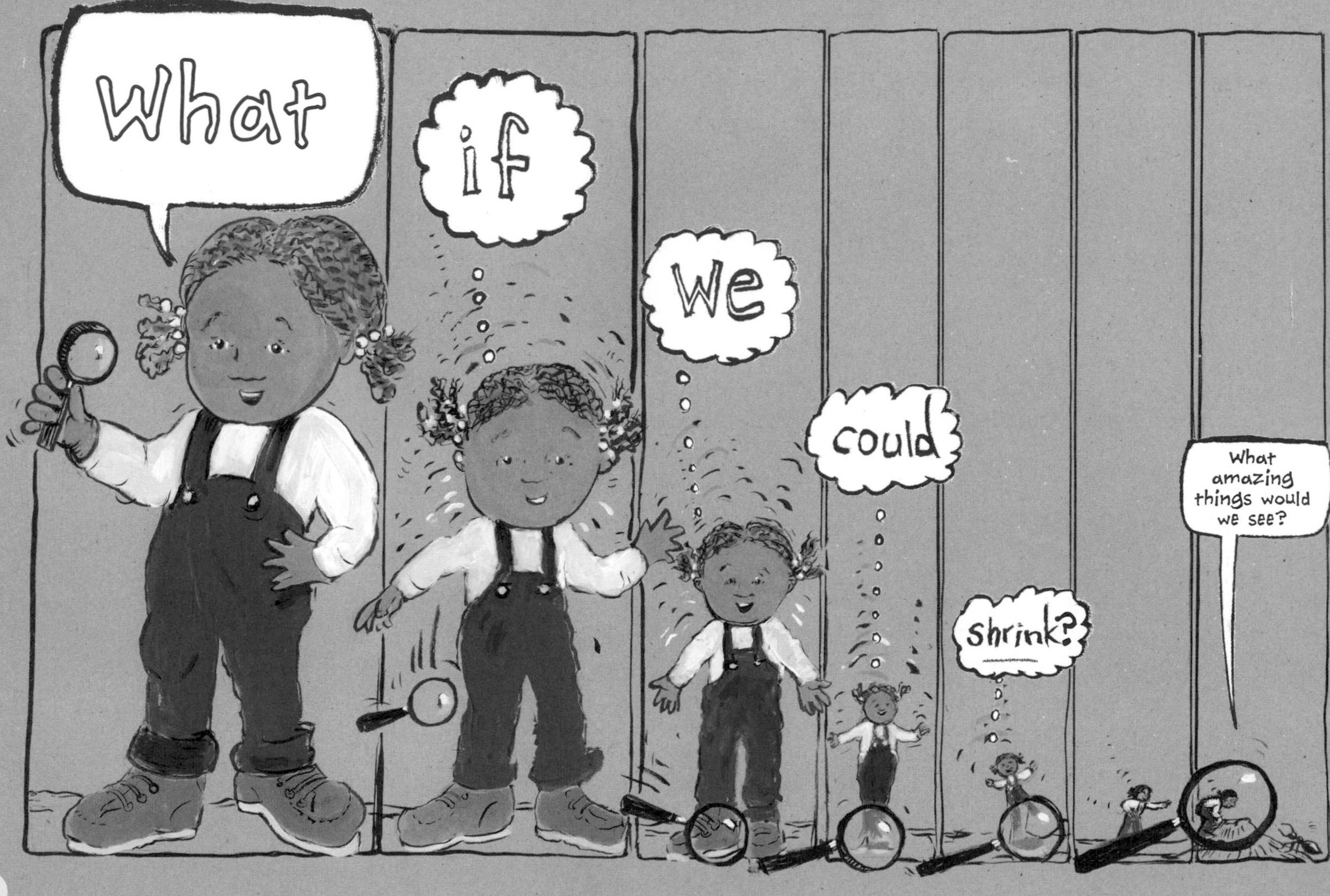
What
if
we
could
shrink?
What amazing things would we see?

CLOSE-UP OF AN ANT

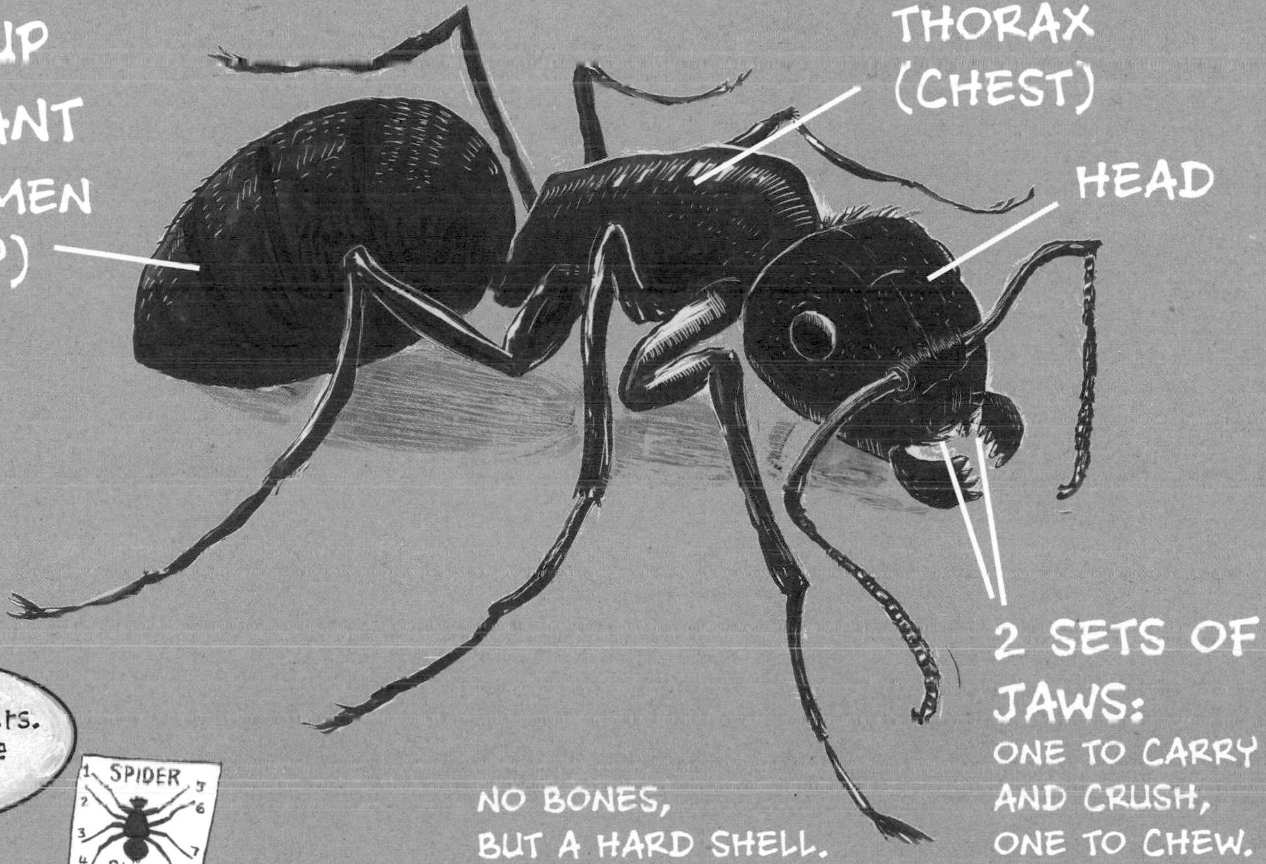

ABDOMEN (BELLY)
THORAX (CHEST)
HEAD
2 SETS OF JAWS:
ONE TO CARRY AND CRUSH, ONE TO CHEW.
NO BONES, BUT A HARD SHELL.

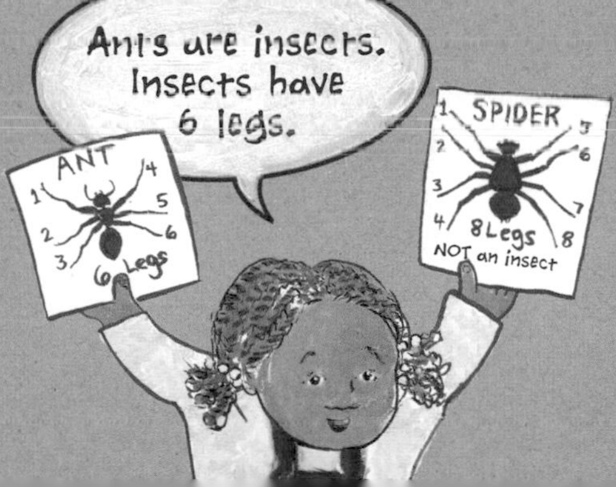

Ants are insects. Insects have 6 legs.
ANT
1 2 3 4 5 6
6 Legs
SPIDER
1 2 3 4 5 6 7 8
8 Legs
NOT an insect

ANTS HAVE TWO STOMACHS.
ONE IS JUST FOR SHARING.

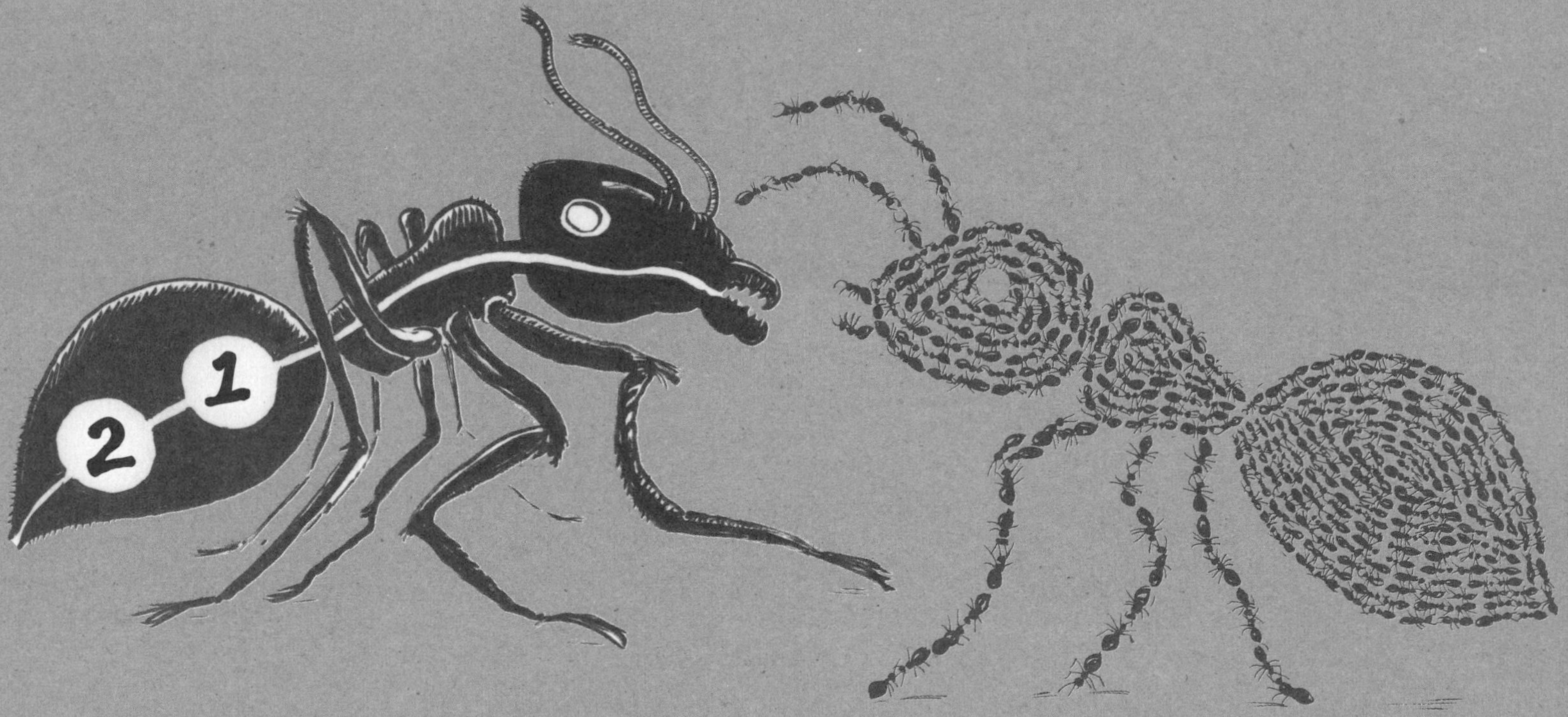

1
2

THEY SHARE FOOD WITH THE WHOLE COLONY.

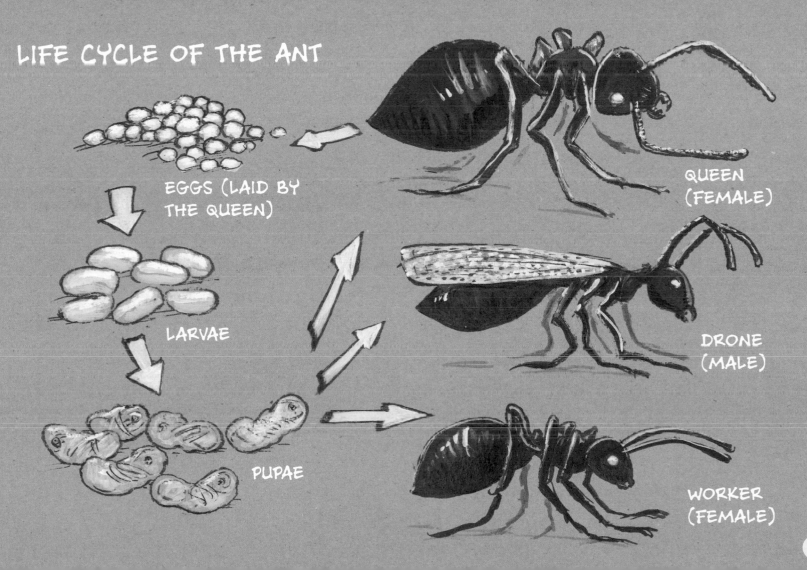

LIFE CYCLE OF THE ANT

EGGS (LAID BY THE QUEEN)

LARVAE

PUPAE

QUEEN (FEMALE)

DRONE (MALE)

WORKER (FEMALE)

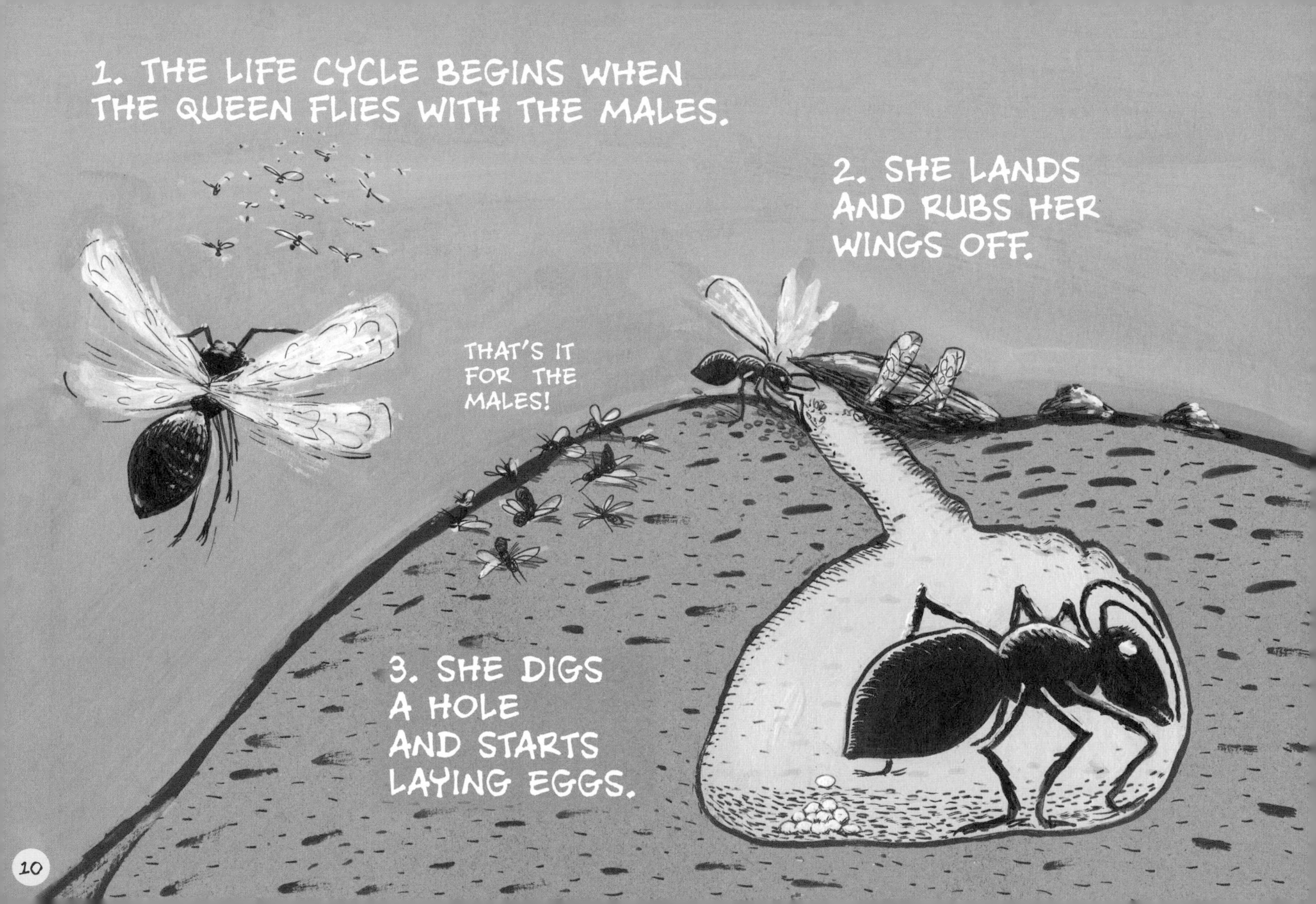
1. THE LIFE CYCLE BEGINS WHEN THE QUEEN FLIES WITH THE MALES.
2. SHE LANDS AND RUBS HER WINGS OFF.
THAT'S IT FOR THE MALES!
3. SHE DIGS A HOLE AND STARTS LAYING EGGS.

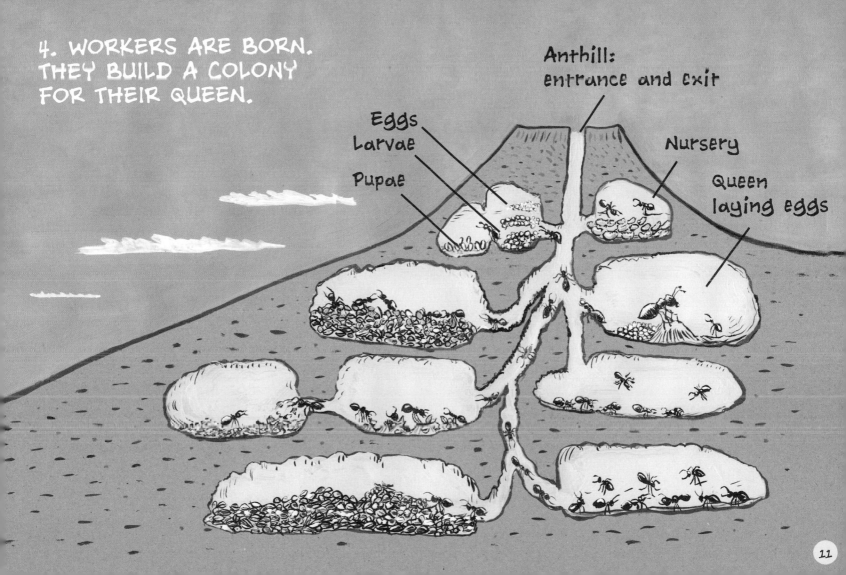

4. WORKERS ARE BORN. THEY BUILD A COLONY FOR THEIR QUEEN.

Anthill: entrance and exit

Eggs
Larvae
Pupae

Nursery

Queen laying eggs

ANTS DON'T SEE WELL, BUT THEY USE FOUR SENSES:

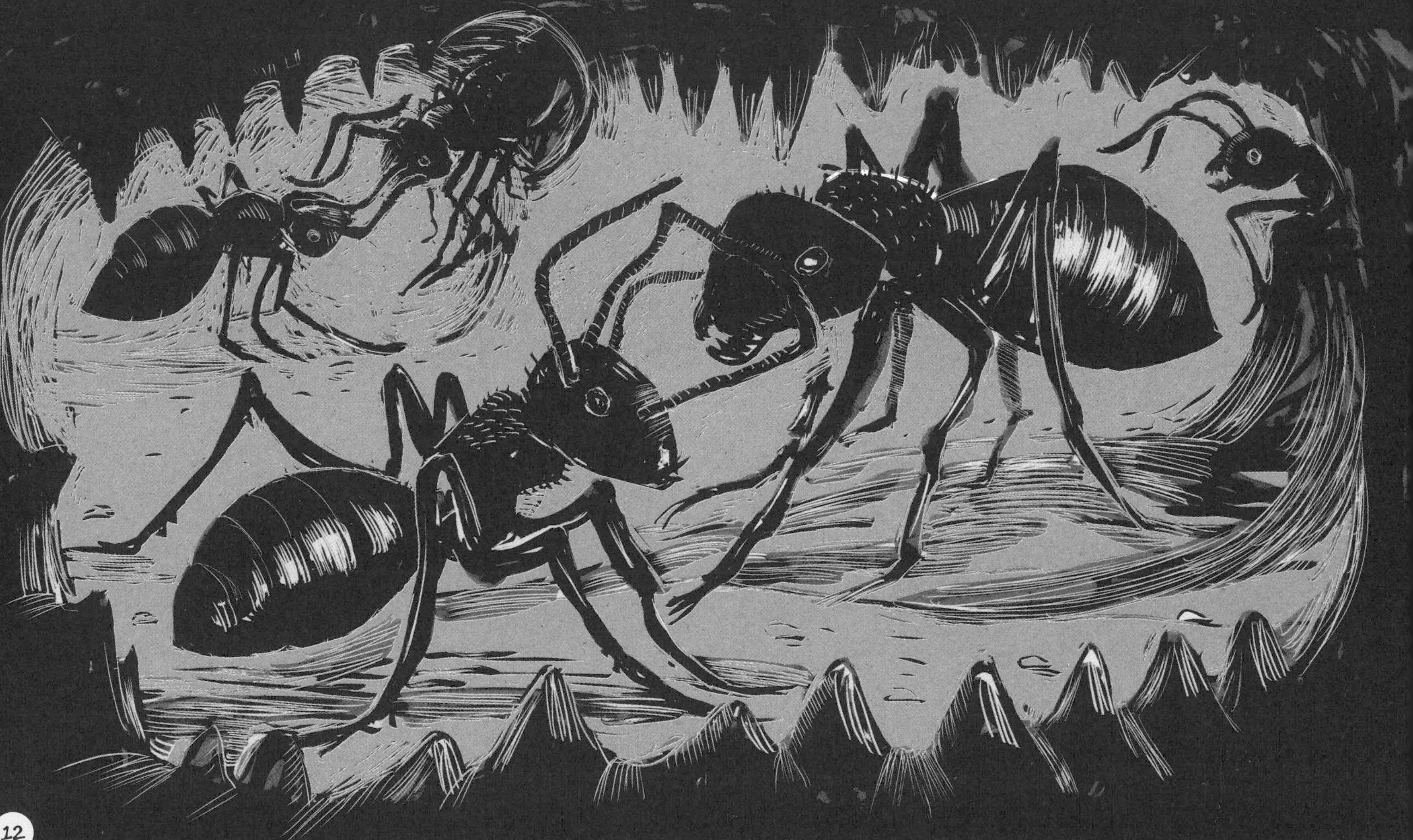

THEY TAP EACH OTHER WITH THEIR ANTENNAE TO SHARE NEWS.

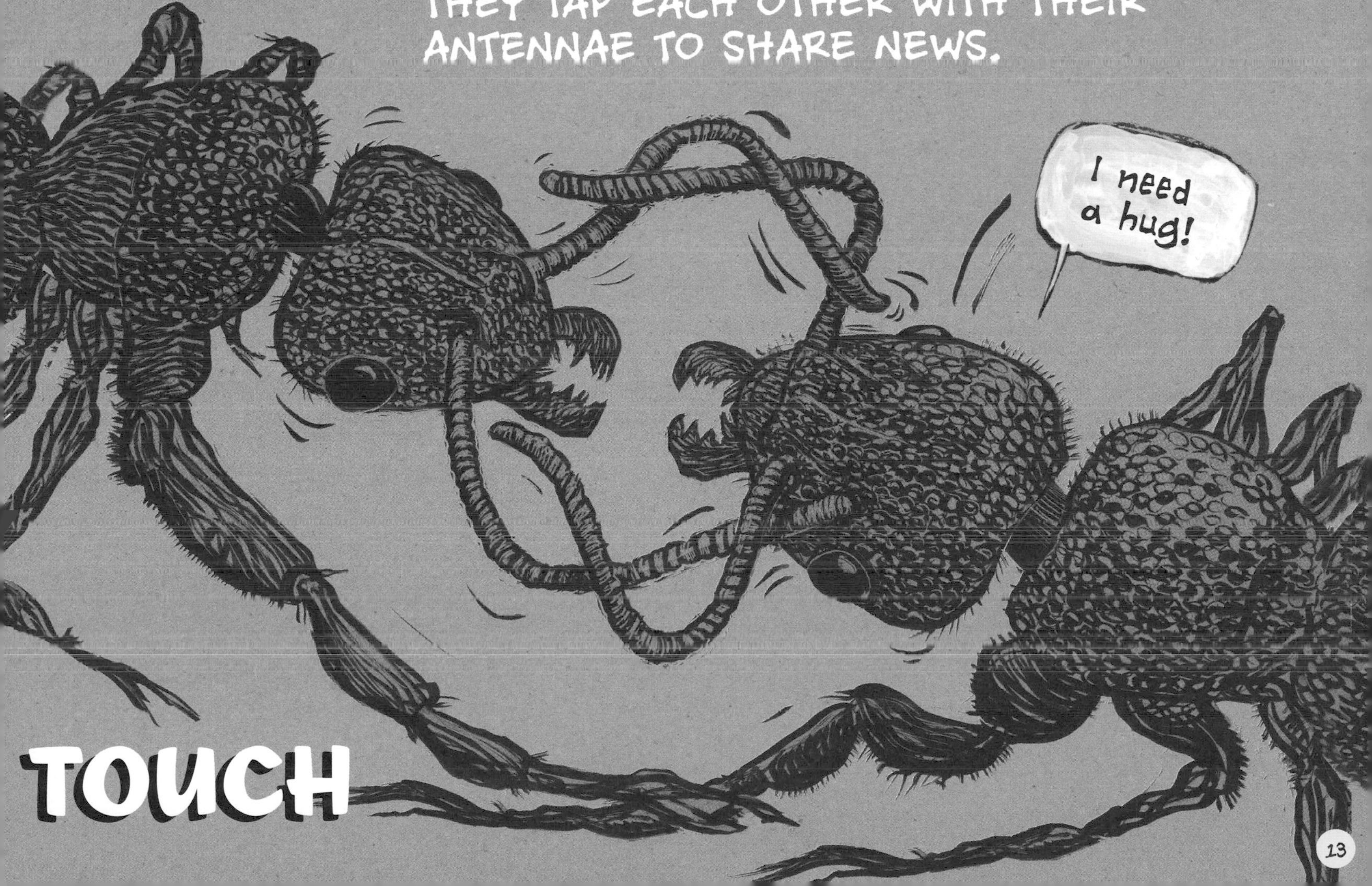
I need a hug!

TOUCH

HEARING

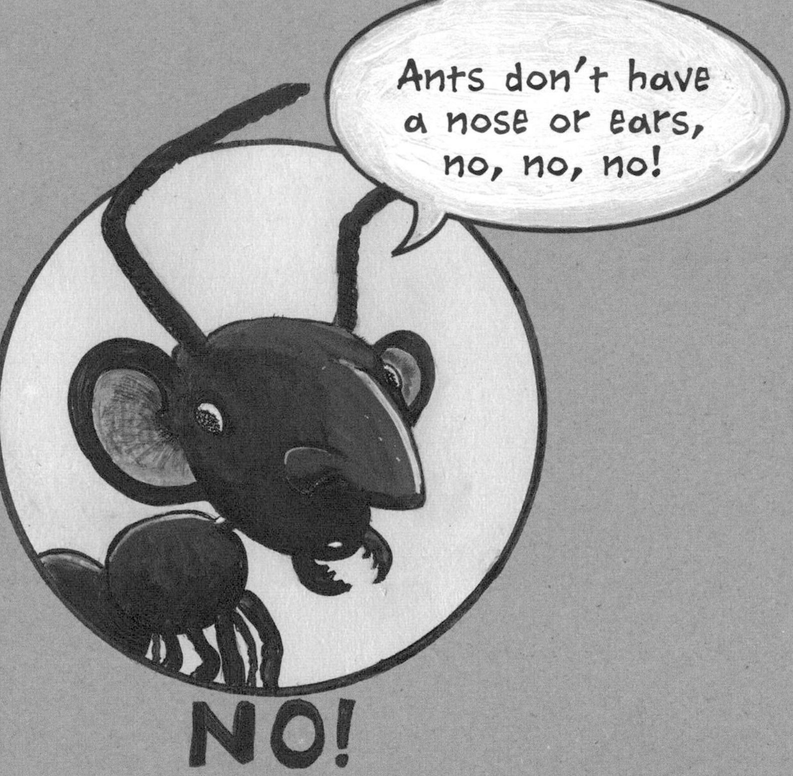

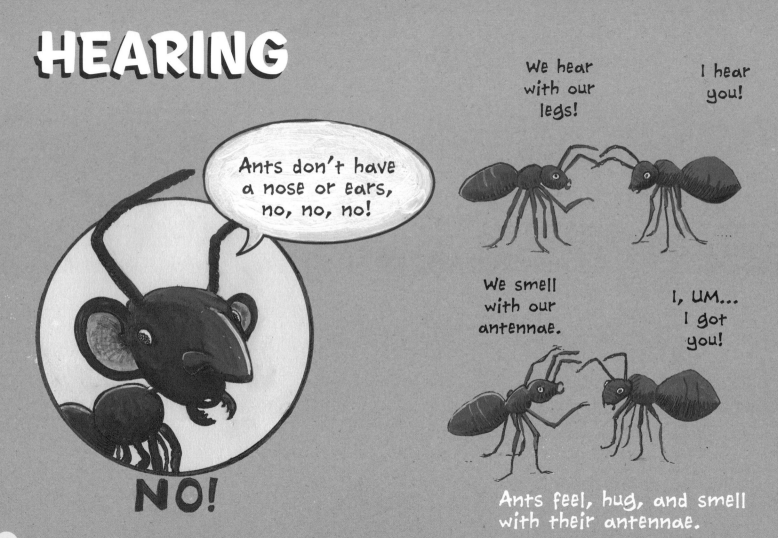

Ants don't have a nose or ears, no, no, no!
NO!

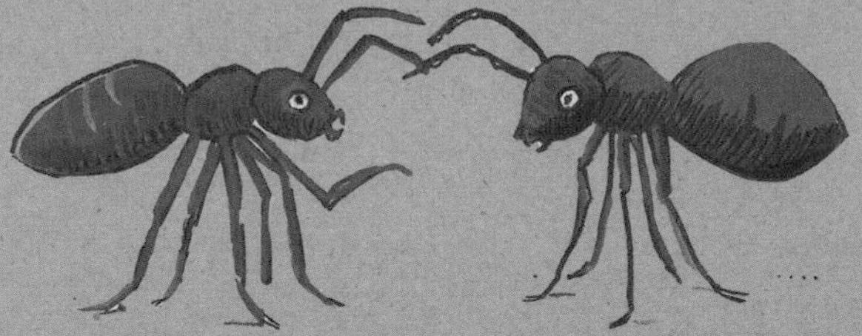

We hear with our legs!
I hear you!

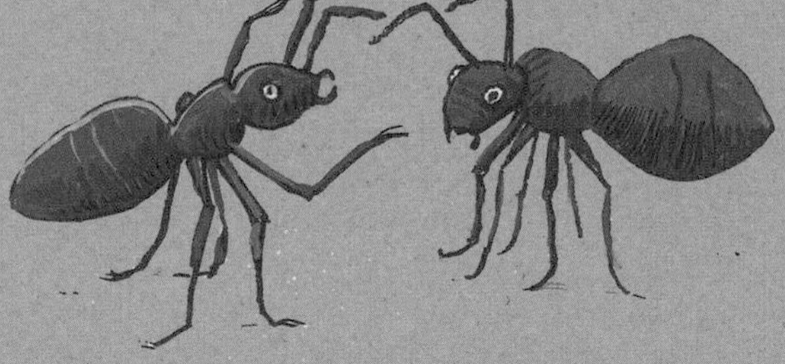

We smell with our antennae.
I, UM... I got you!

Ants feel, hug, and smell with their antennae.

SMELL

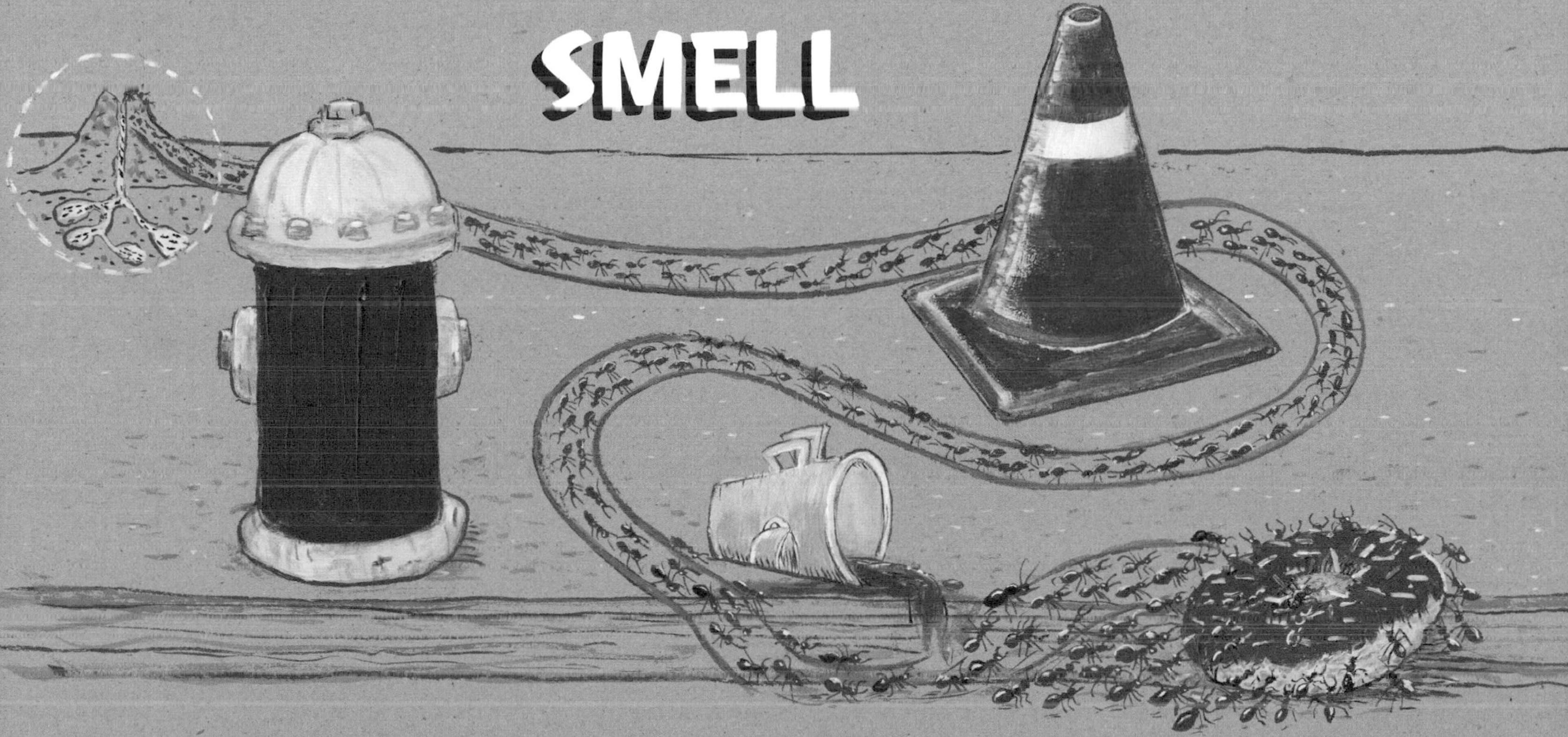

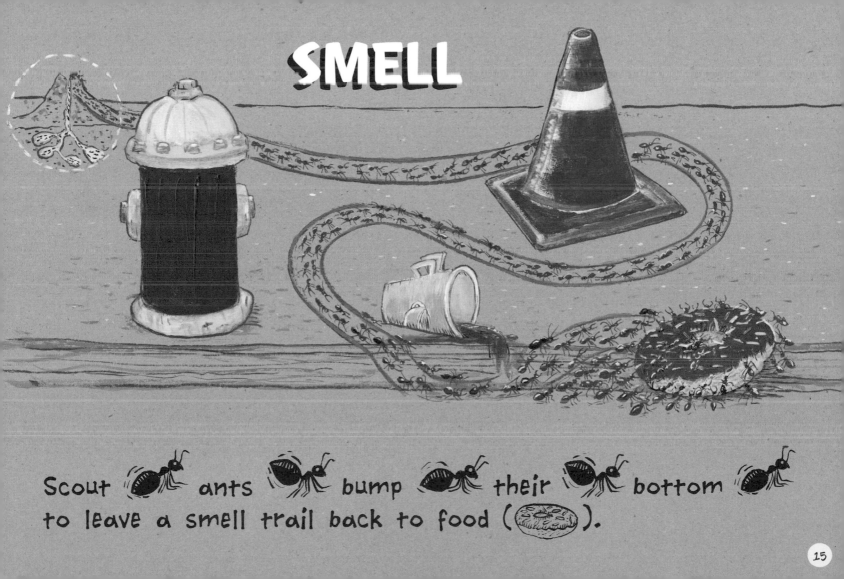

Scout ants bump their bottom to leave a smell trail back to food ( ).

TASTE

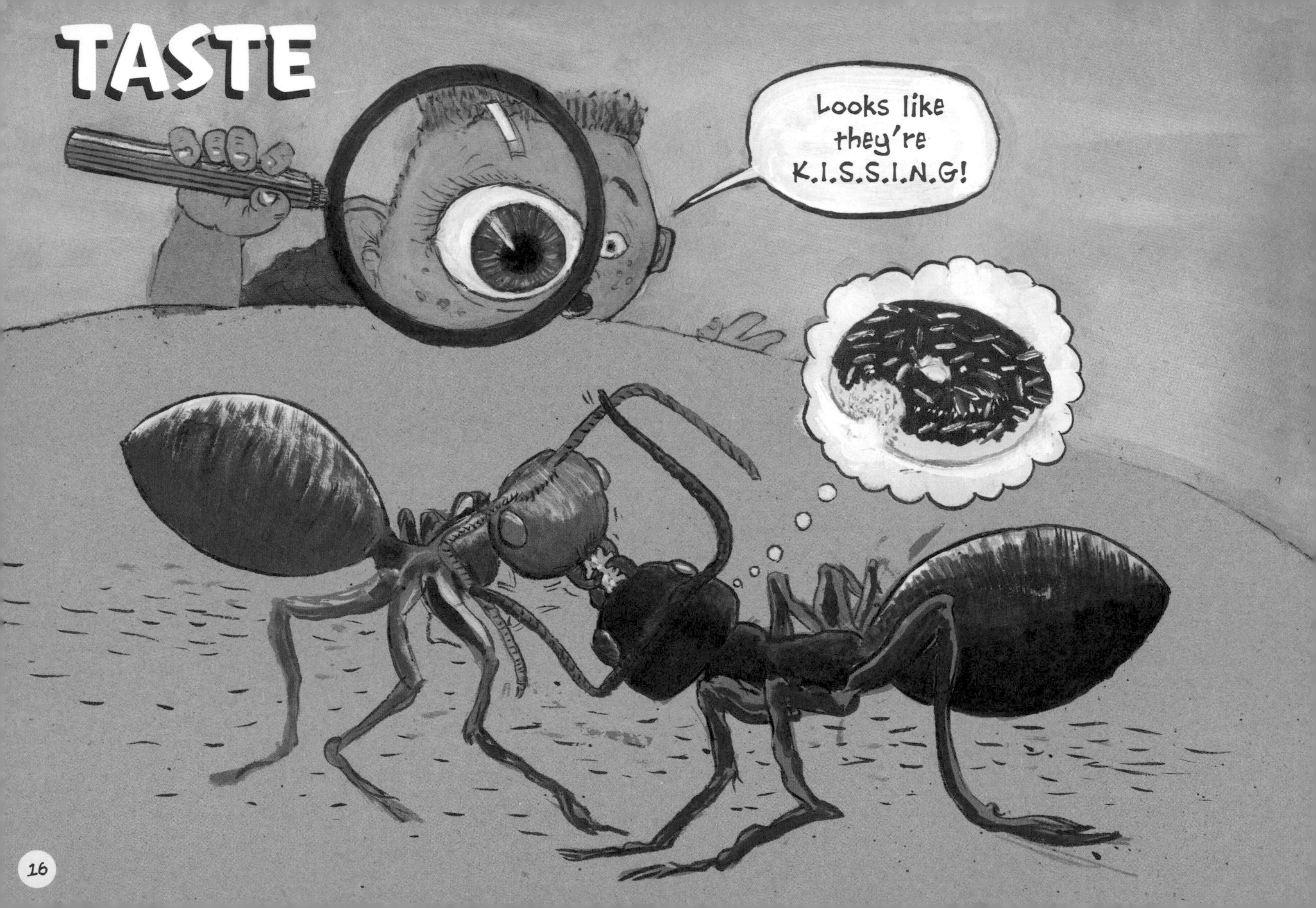
Looks like they're K.I.S.S.I.N.G!

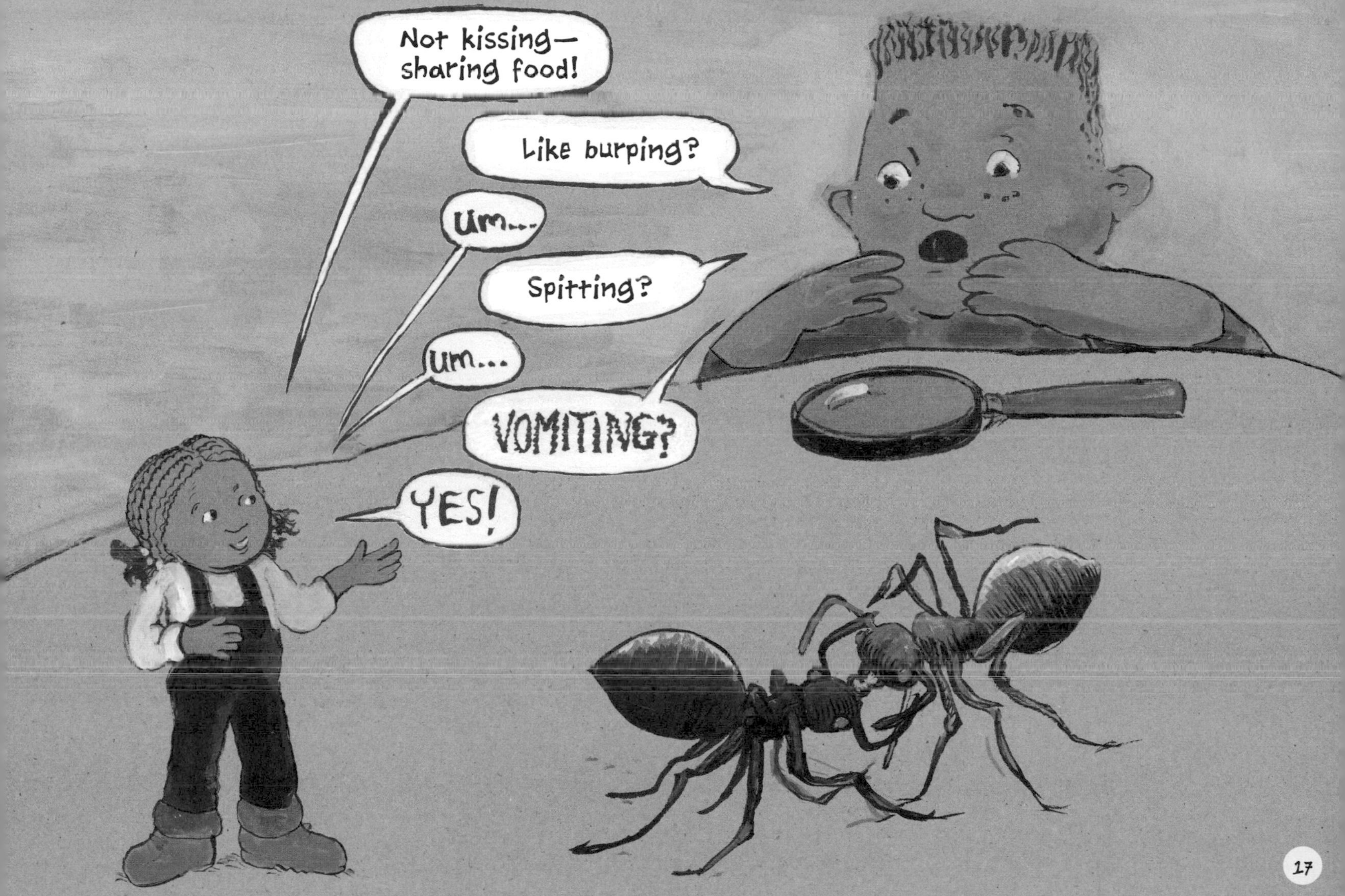
Not kissing—
sharing food!
Like burping?
Um...
Spitting?
Um...
VOMITING?
YES!

THIS IS
1000
ANTS.
SOME
COLONIES
ARE
MUCH
BIGGER.

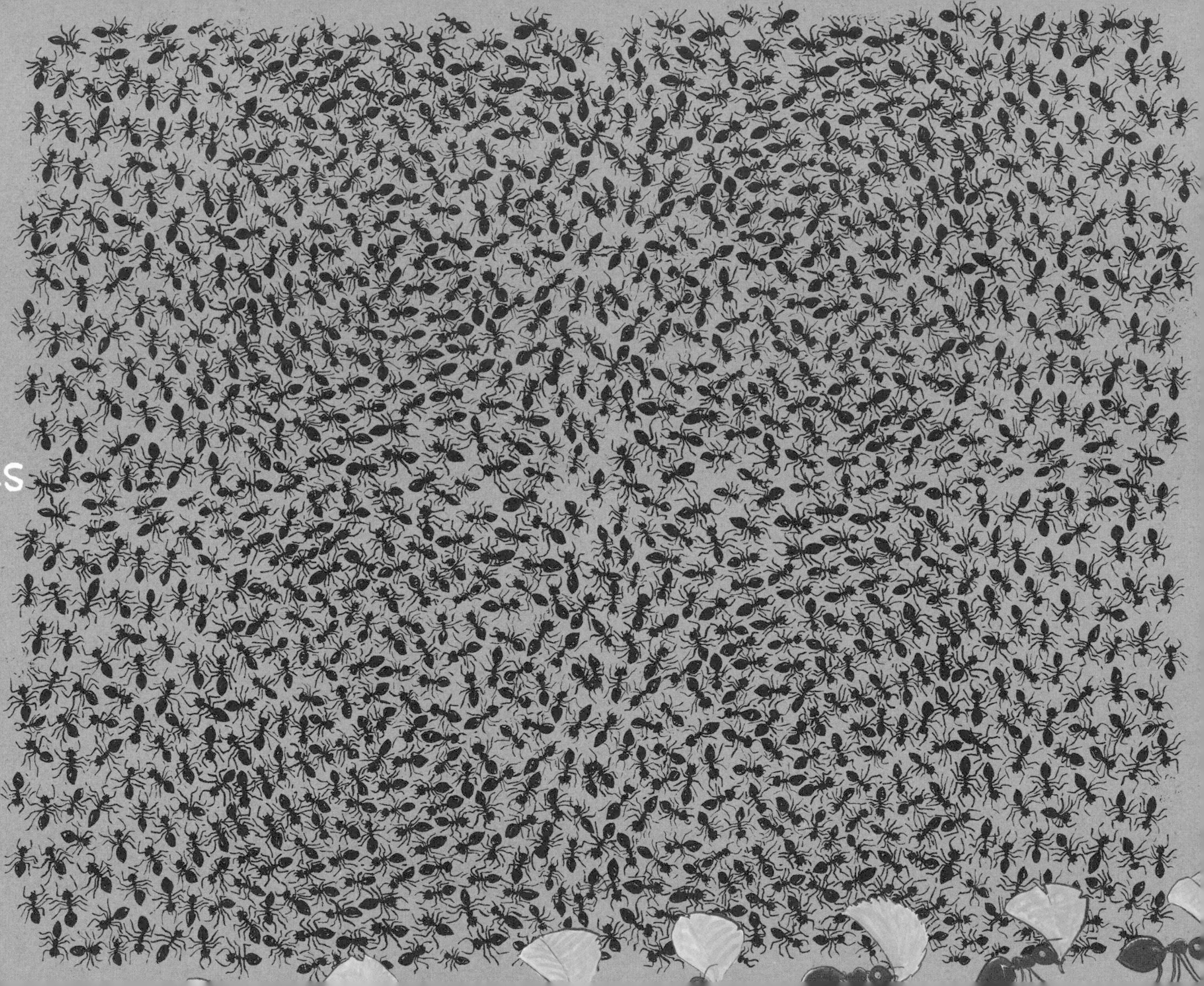

AND THERE ARE THOUSANDS OF KINDS OF ANTS:

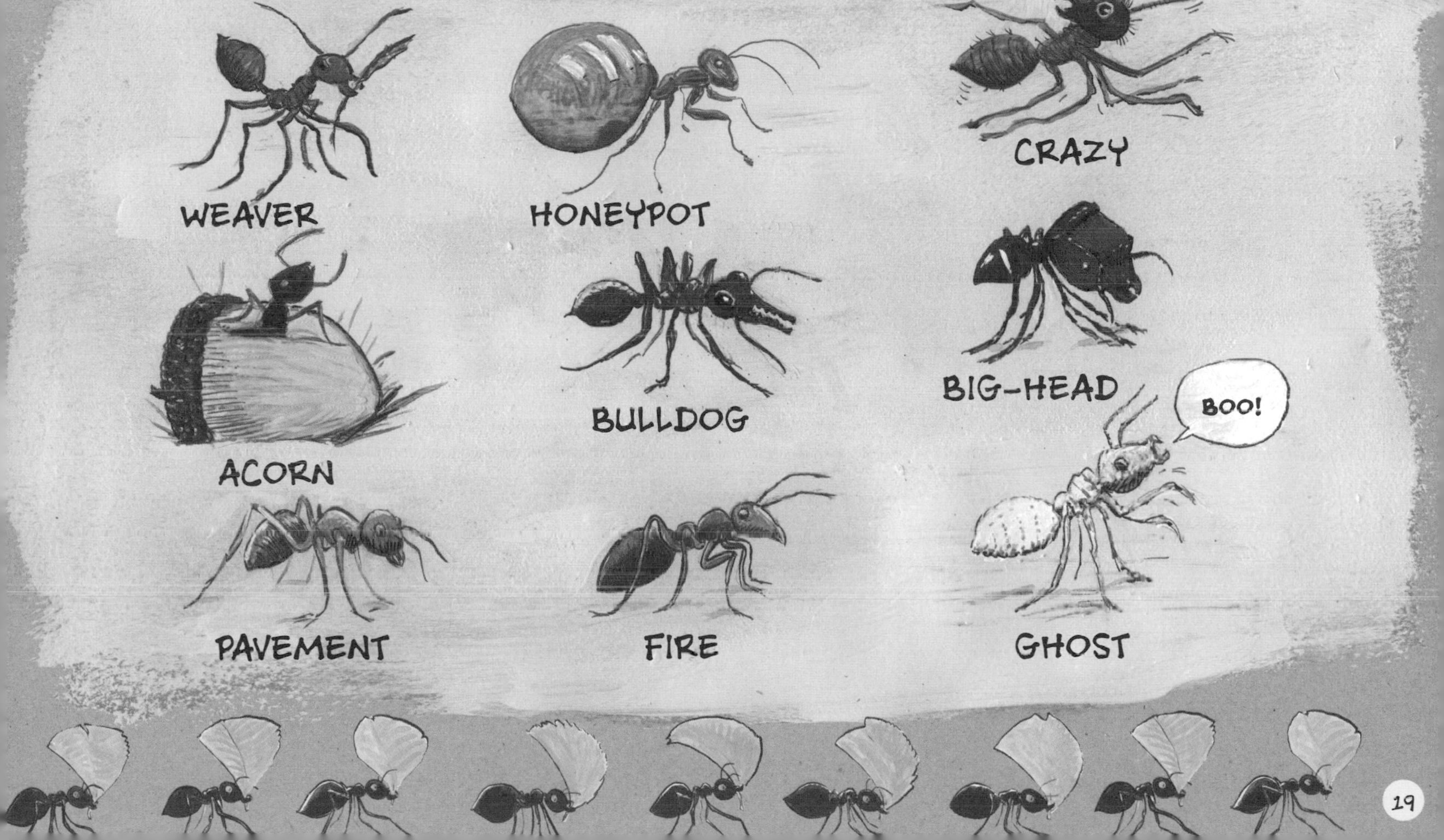
WEAVER
HONEYPOT
CRAZY
ACORN
BULLDOG
BIG-HEAD
BOO!
PAVEMENT
FIRE
GHOST

LEAF-CUTTER ANTS WORK TOGETHER TO FARM.

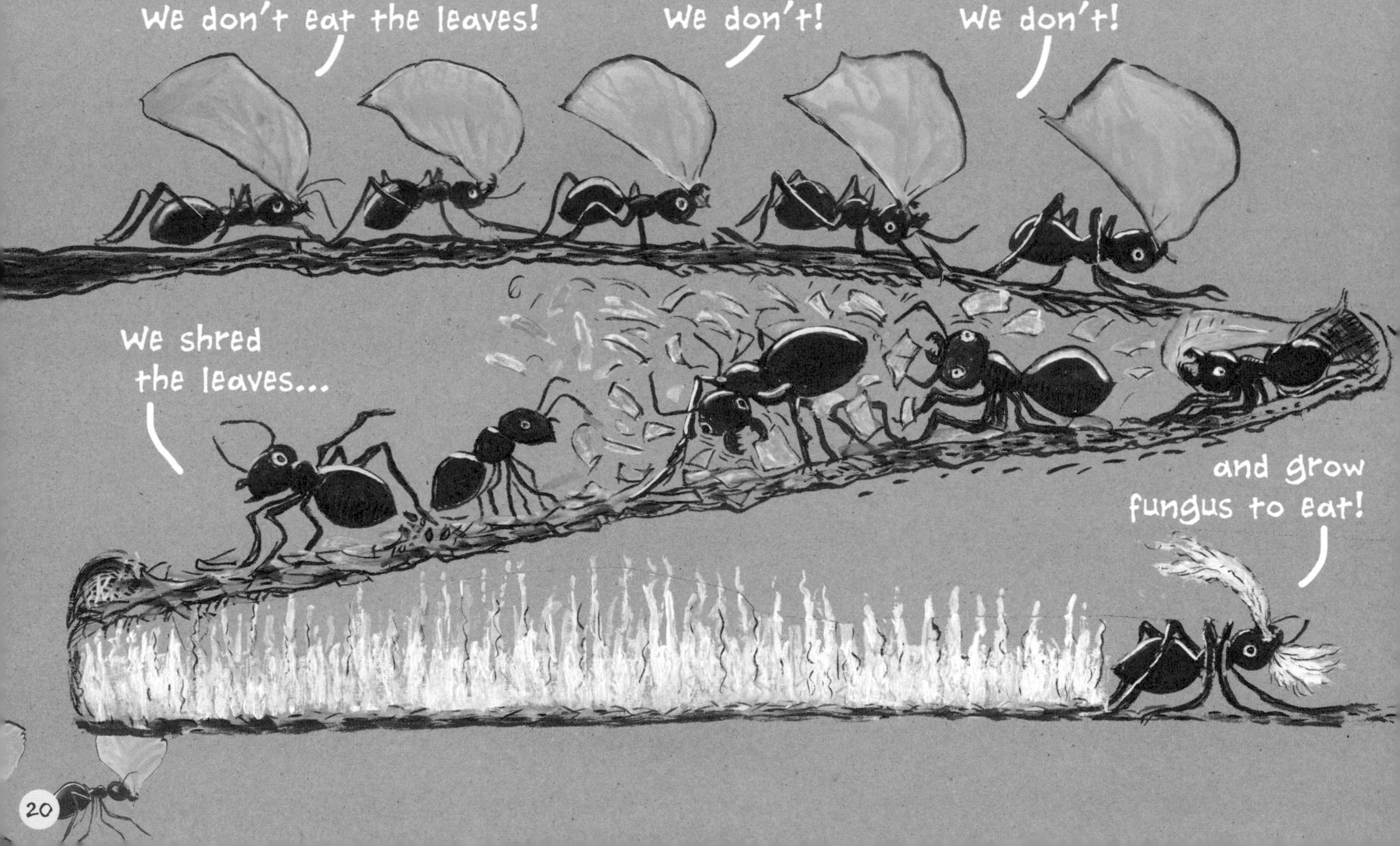
We don't eat the leaves!
We don't!
We don't!
We shred the leaves...
and grow fungus to eat!

SOME ANTS RAISE AND MILK TINY INSECTS.

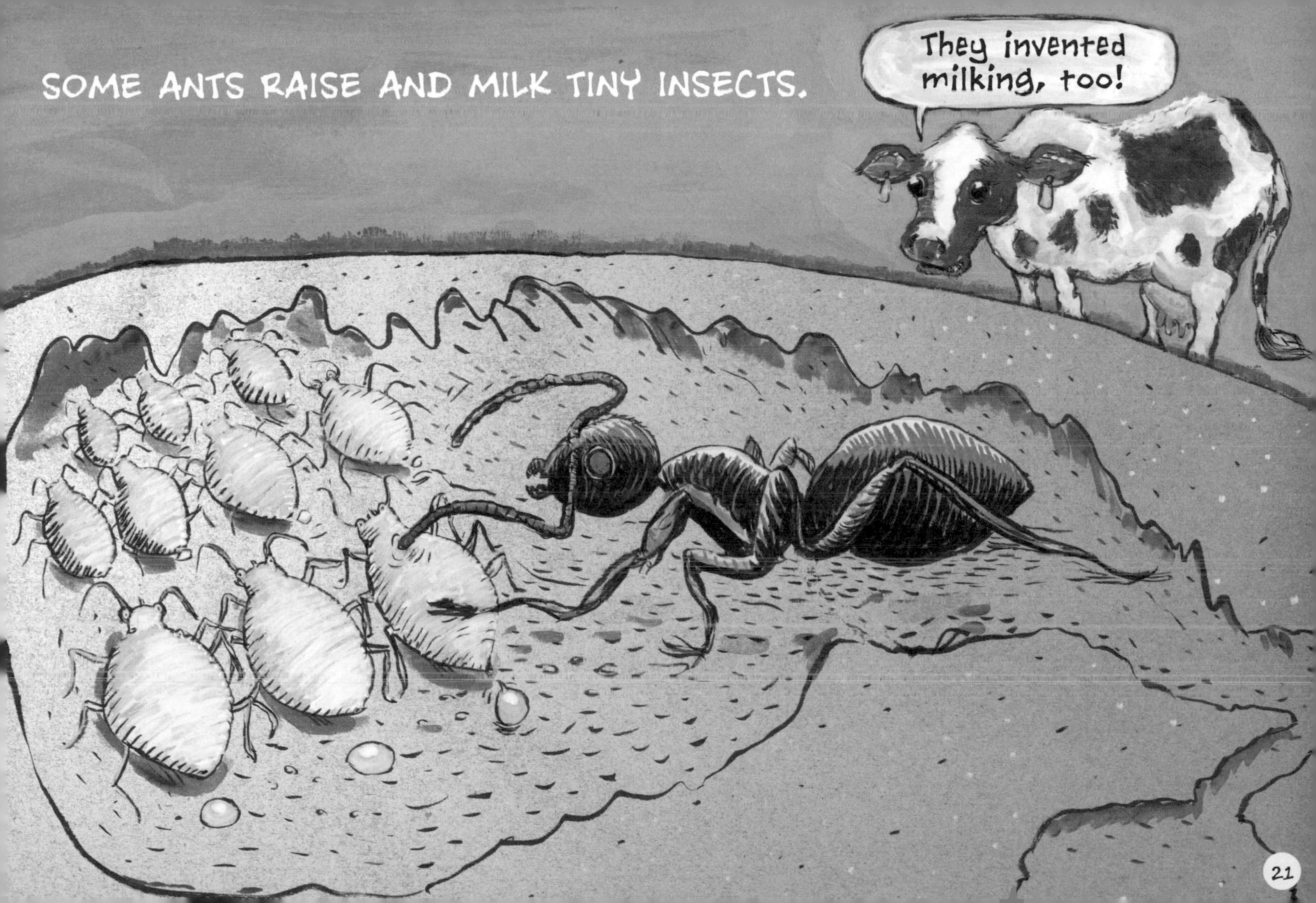
They invented milking, too!

A TRAP-JAW ANT CLOSES
ITS JAWS VERY, VERY FAST.

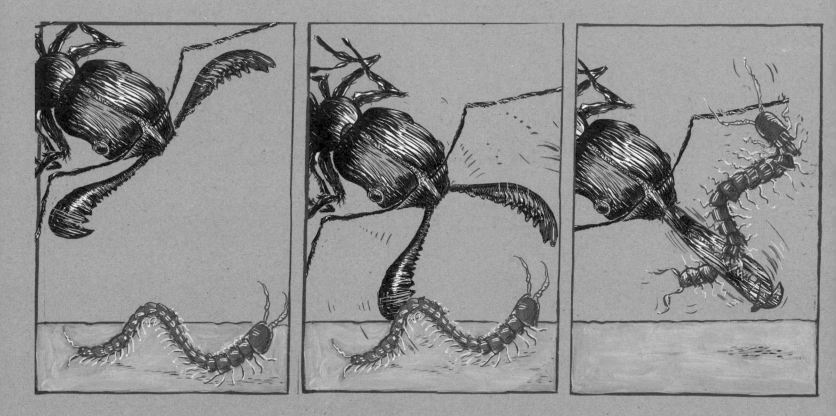

IT CAN ALSO SNAP ITS JAWS QUICKLY TO JUMP AWAY.

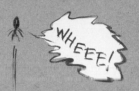

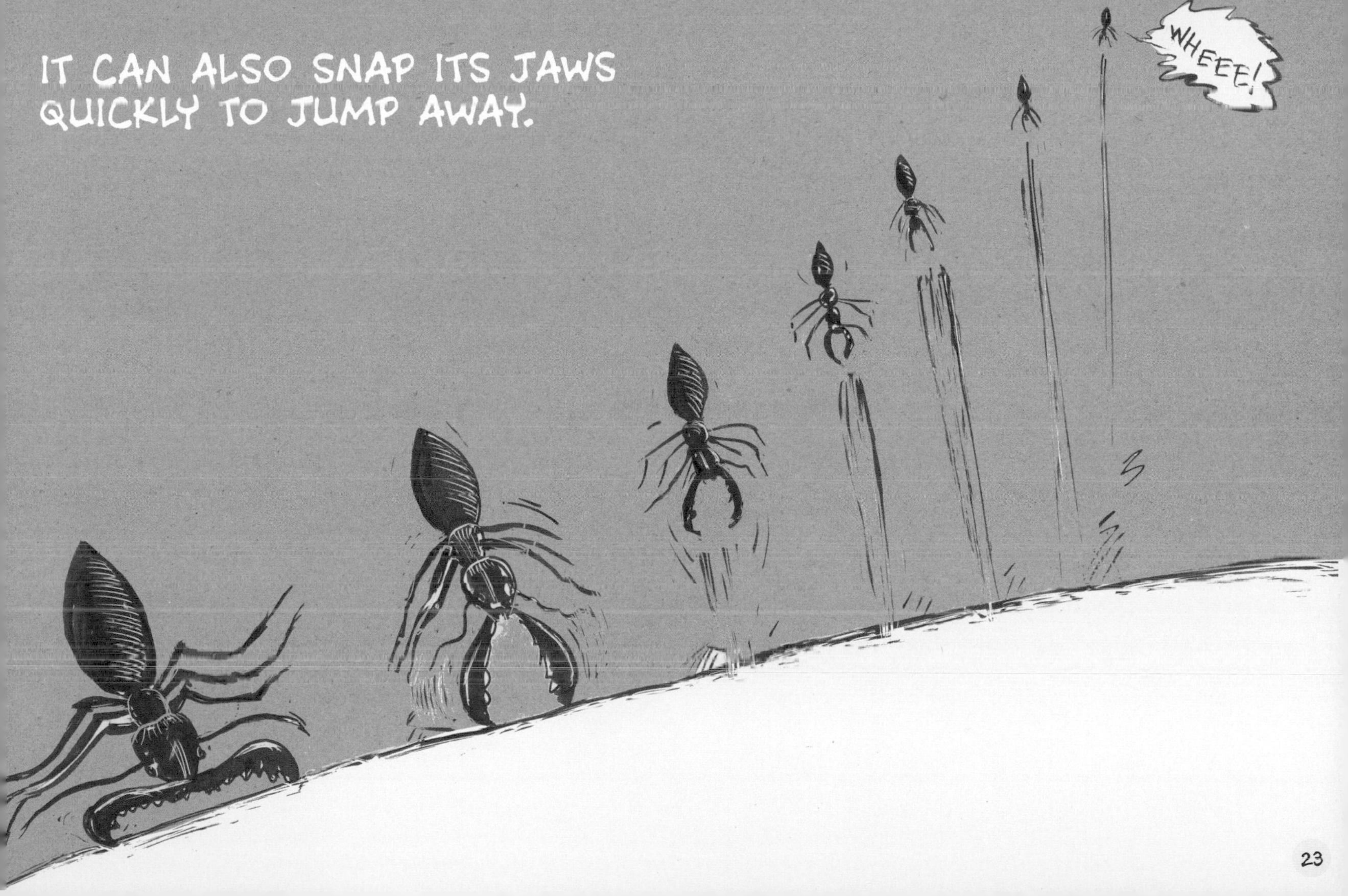
WHEEEE!

ANTS CAN LIFT UP TO 50 TIMES THEIR OWN WEIGHT.

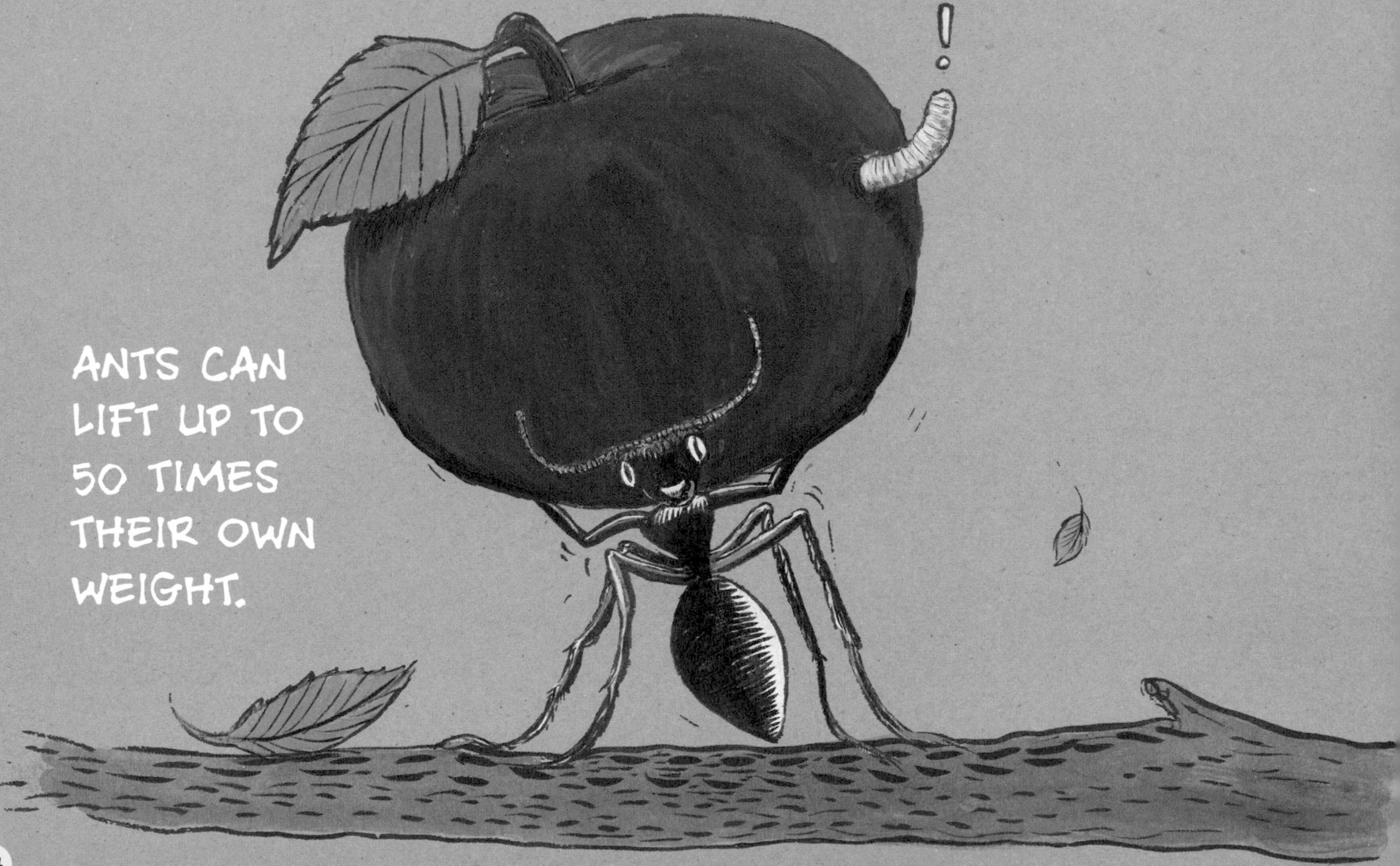

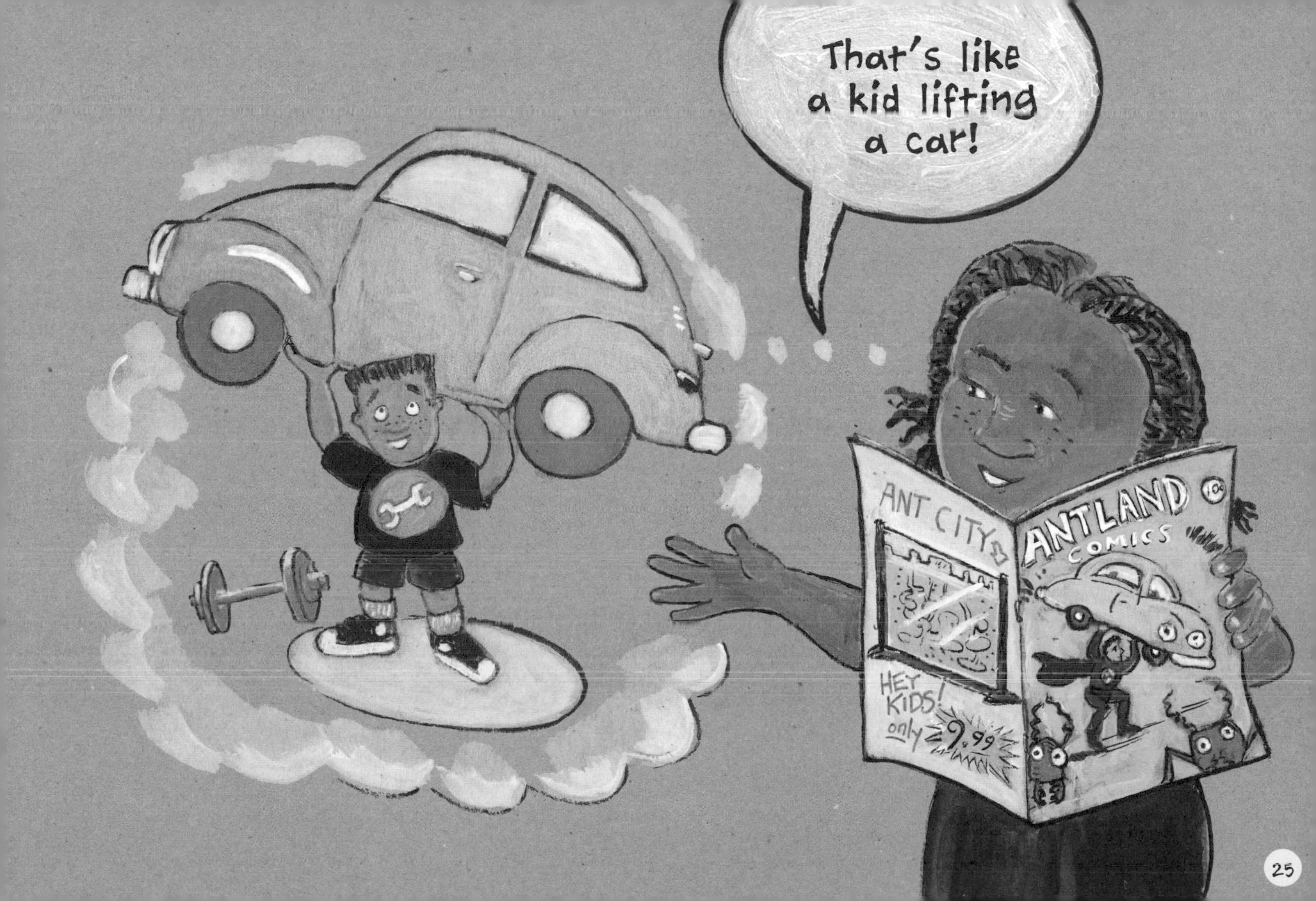
That's like a kid lifting a car!
ANT CITY
ANTLAND COMICS
10¢
HEY KIDS! only 9.99

SOME ANTS LIVE IN TREES. ELEPHANTS ARE SCARED OF THEM.

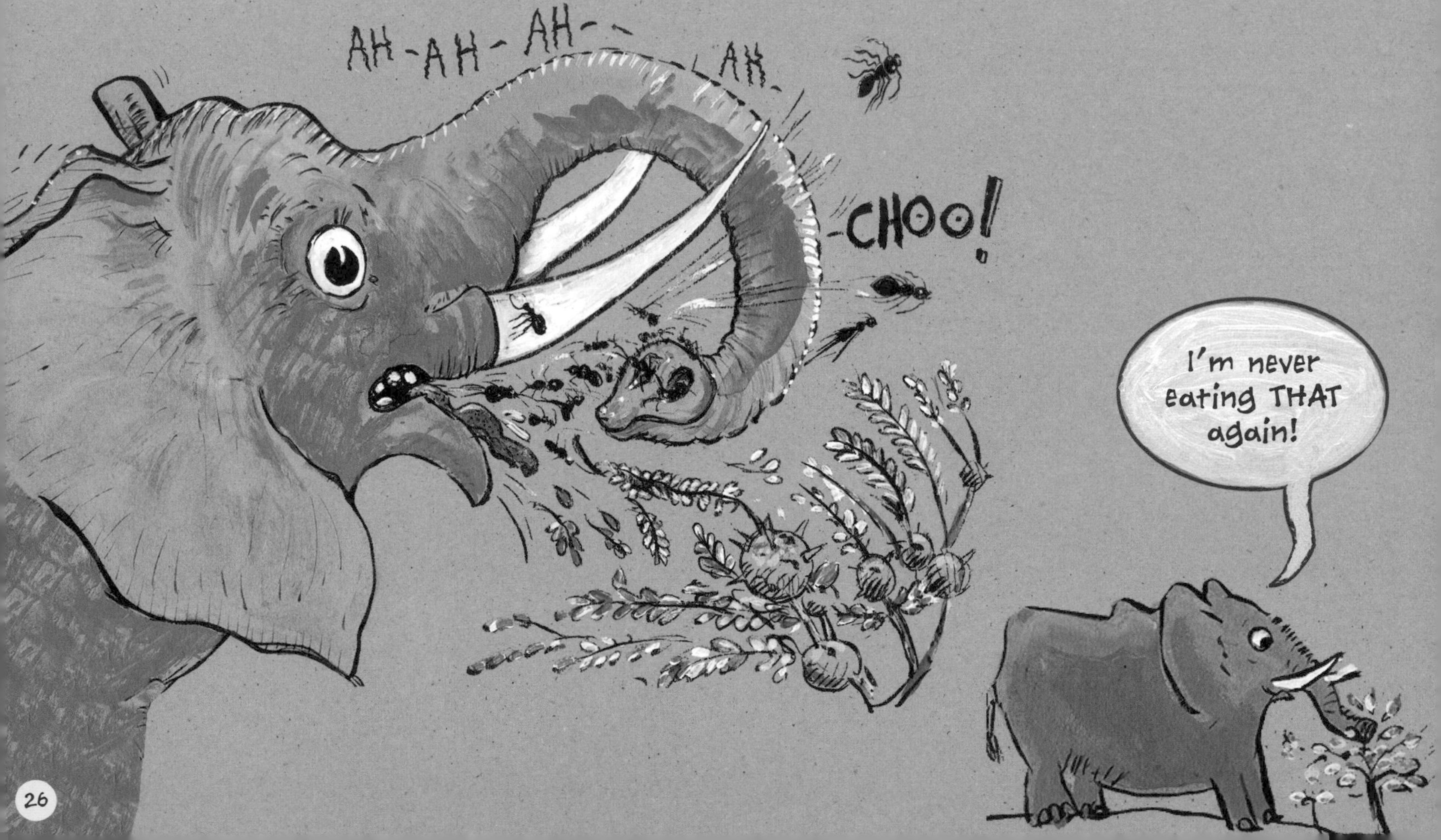
AH-AH-AH-- -AH-
-CHOO!
I'm never eating THAT again!

TO PROTECT THE COLONY,

EXPLODING ANTS ACTUALLY EXPLODE!

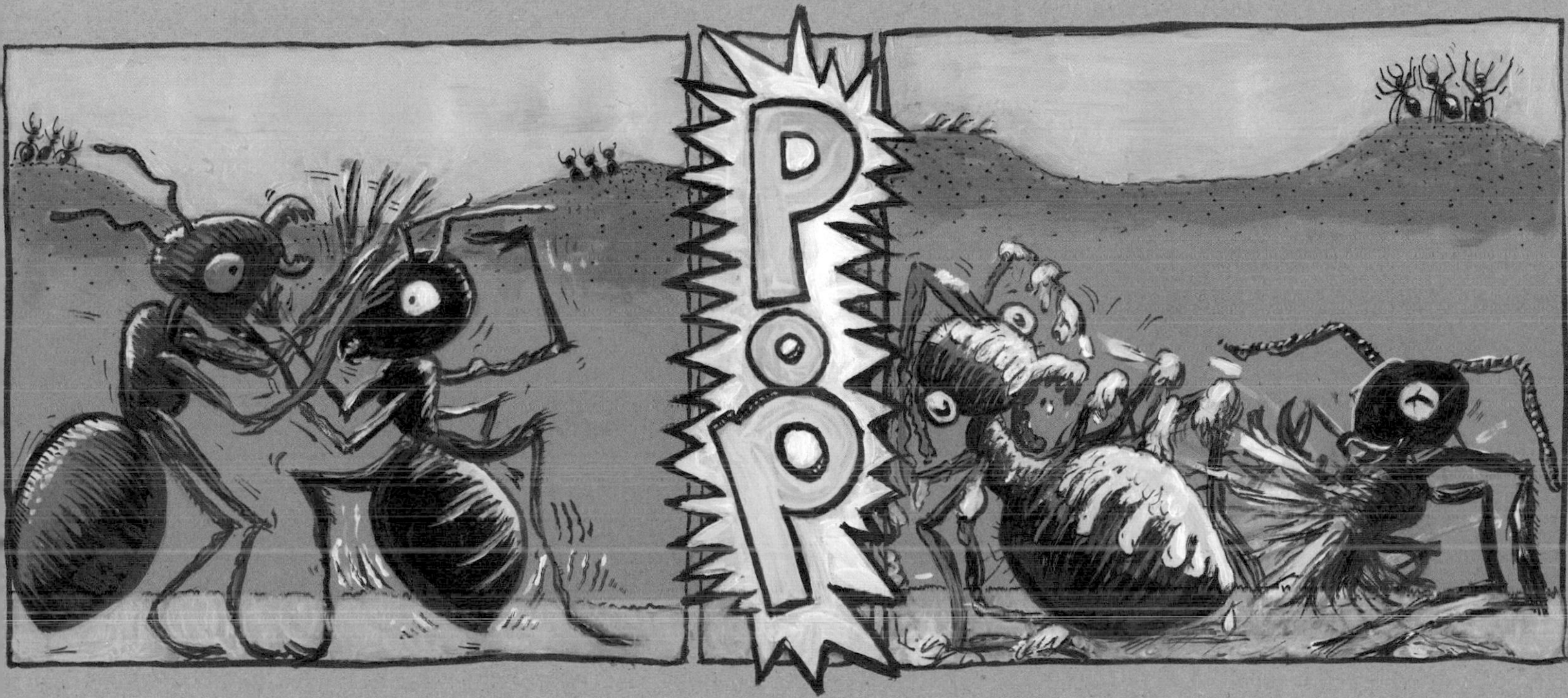
POP

THEY COVER THEIR ENEMY IN YELLOW GOO.

WHAT ANTS EAT...

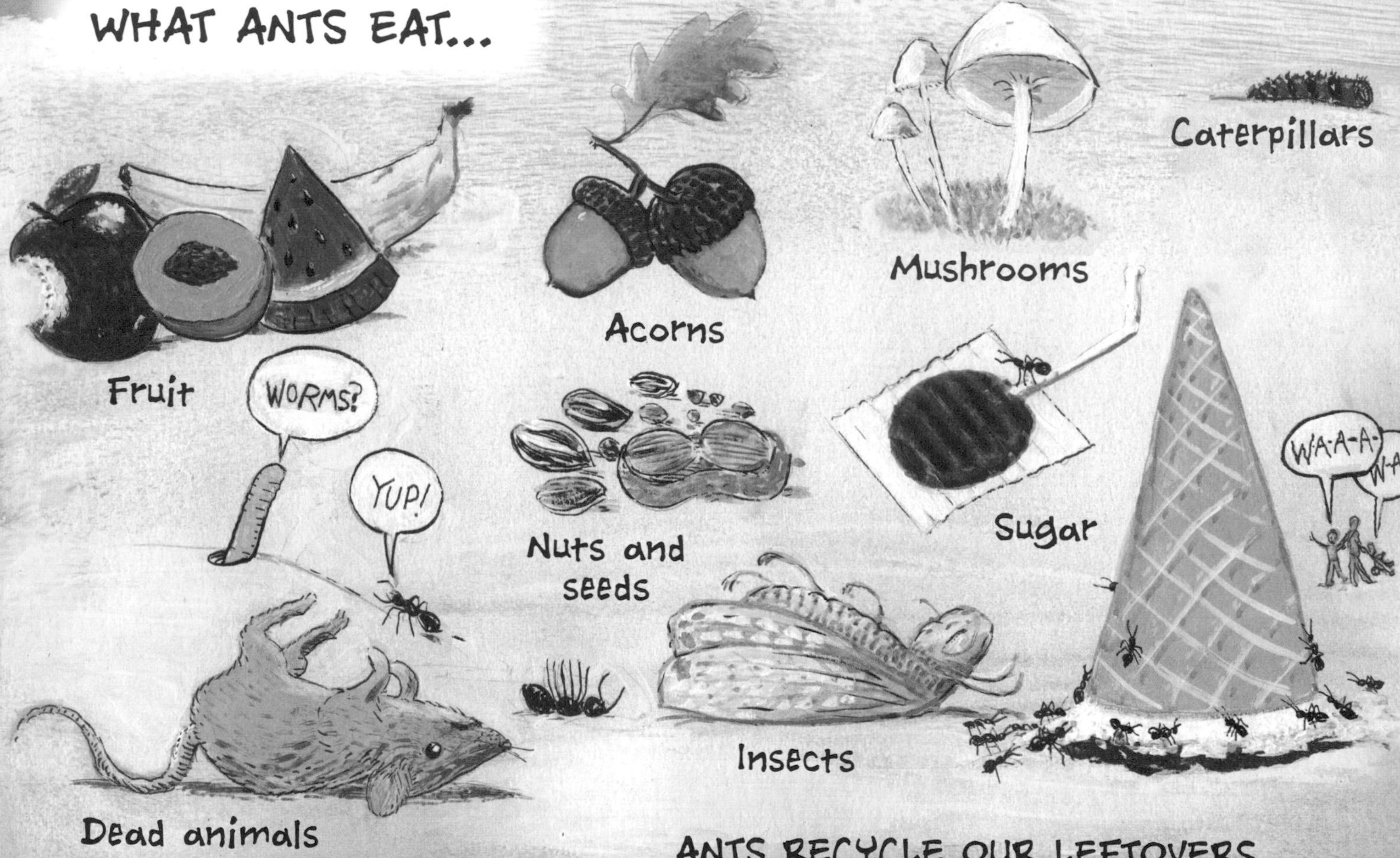

Fruit
WORMS?
YUP!
Acorns
Nuts and seeds
Mushrooms
Caterpillars
Sugar
W-A-A-A-
W-A-A!
Insects
Dead animals

ANTS RECYCLE OUR LEFTOVERS.

WHAT EATS ANTS...

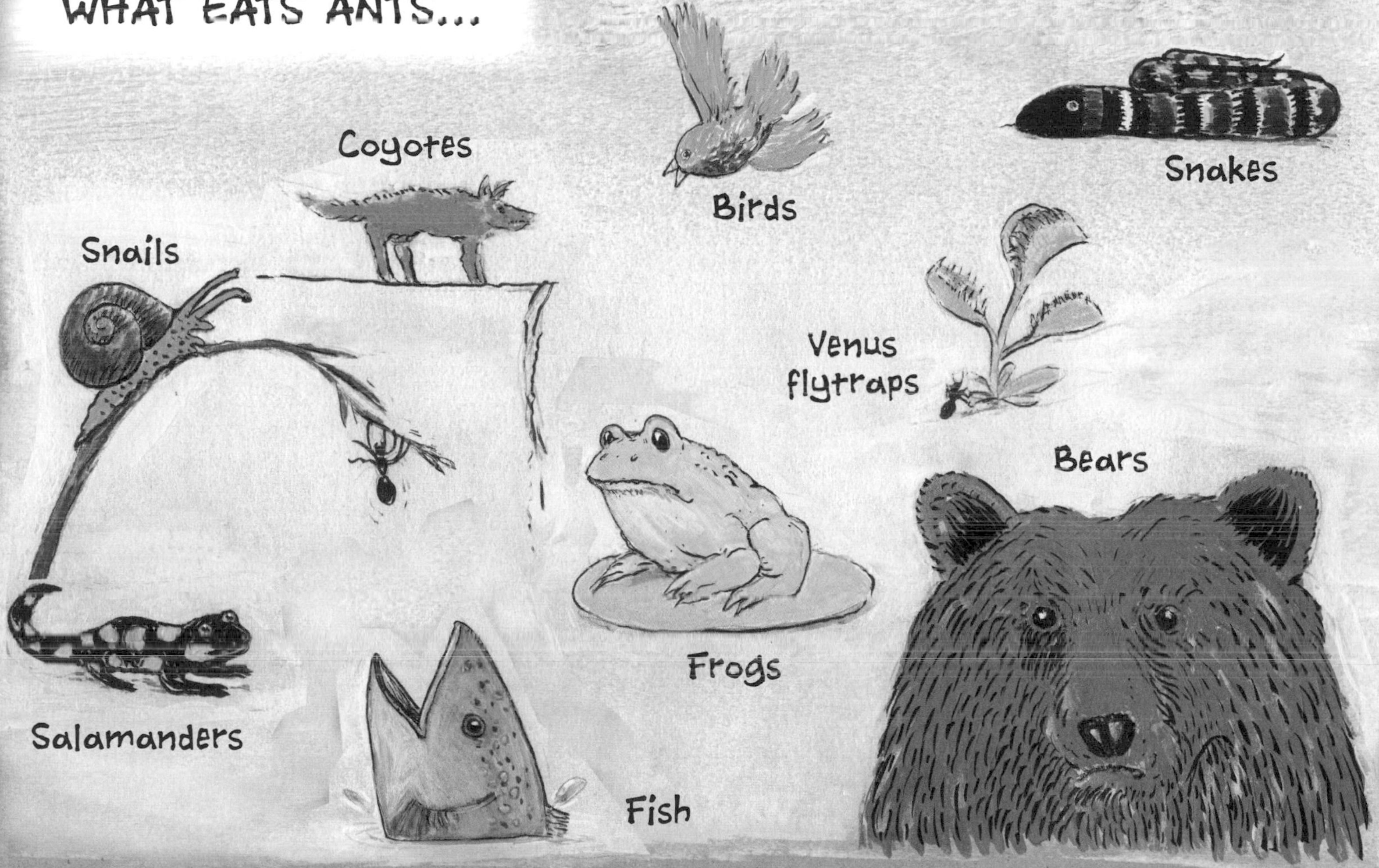
Coyotes
Birds
Snakes
Snails
Venus flytraps
Bears
Frogs
Salamanders
Fish

LET'S NOT FORGET ANTEATERS!

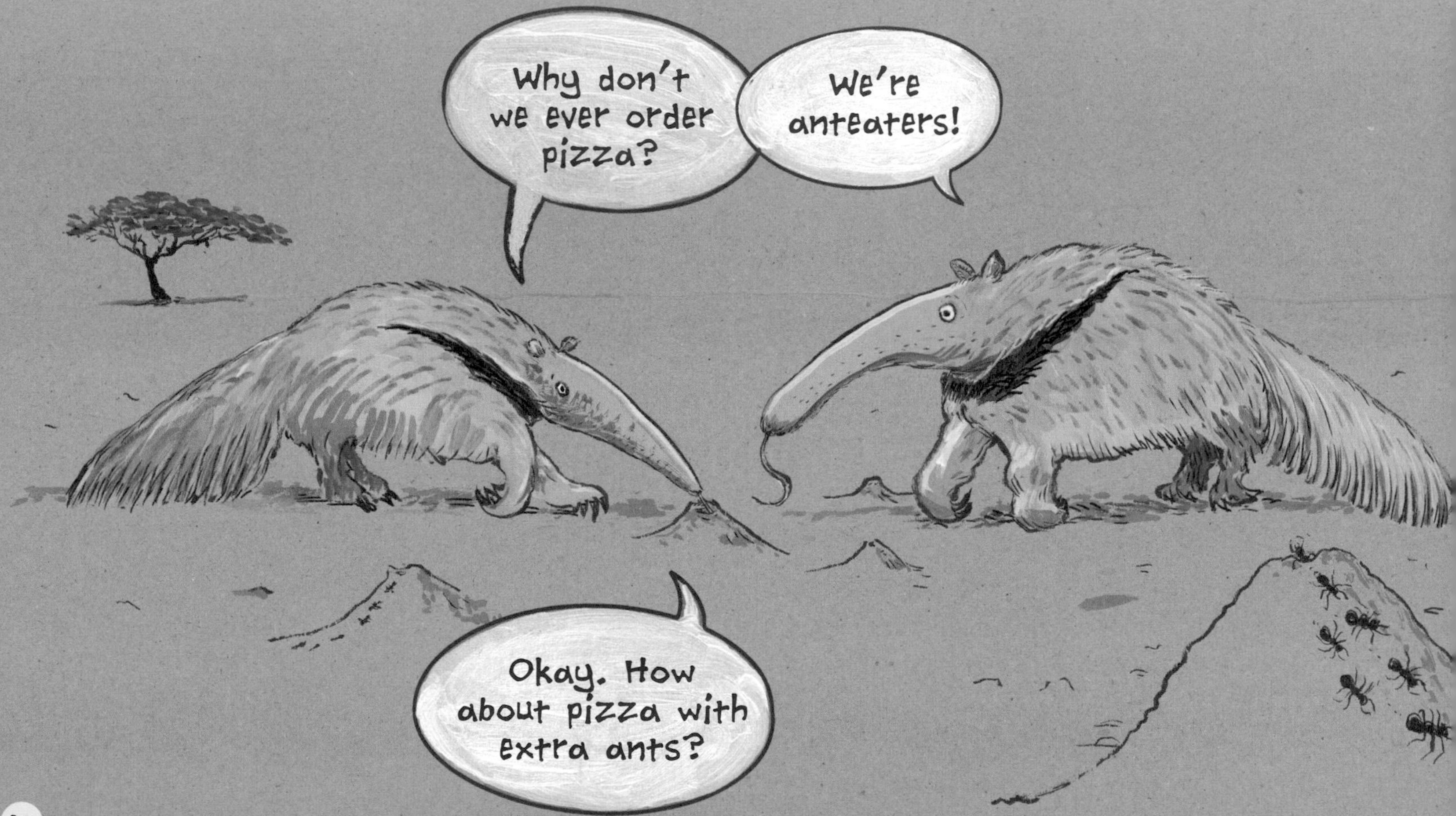
Why don't we ever order pizza?
We're anteaters!
Okay. How about pizza with extra ants?

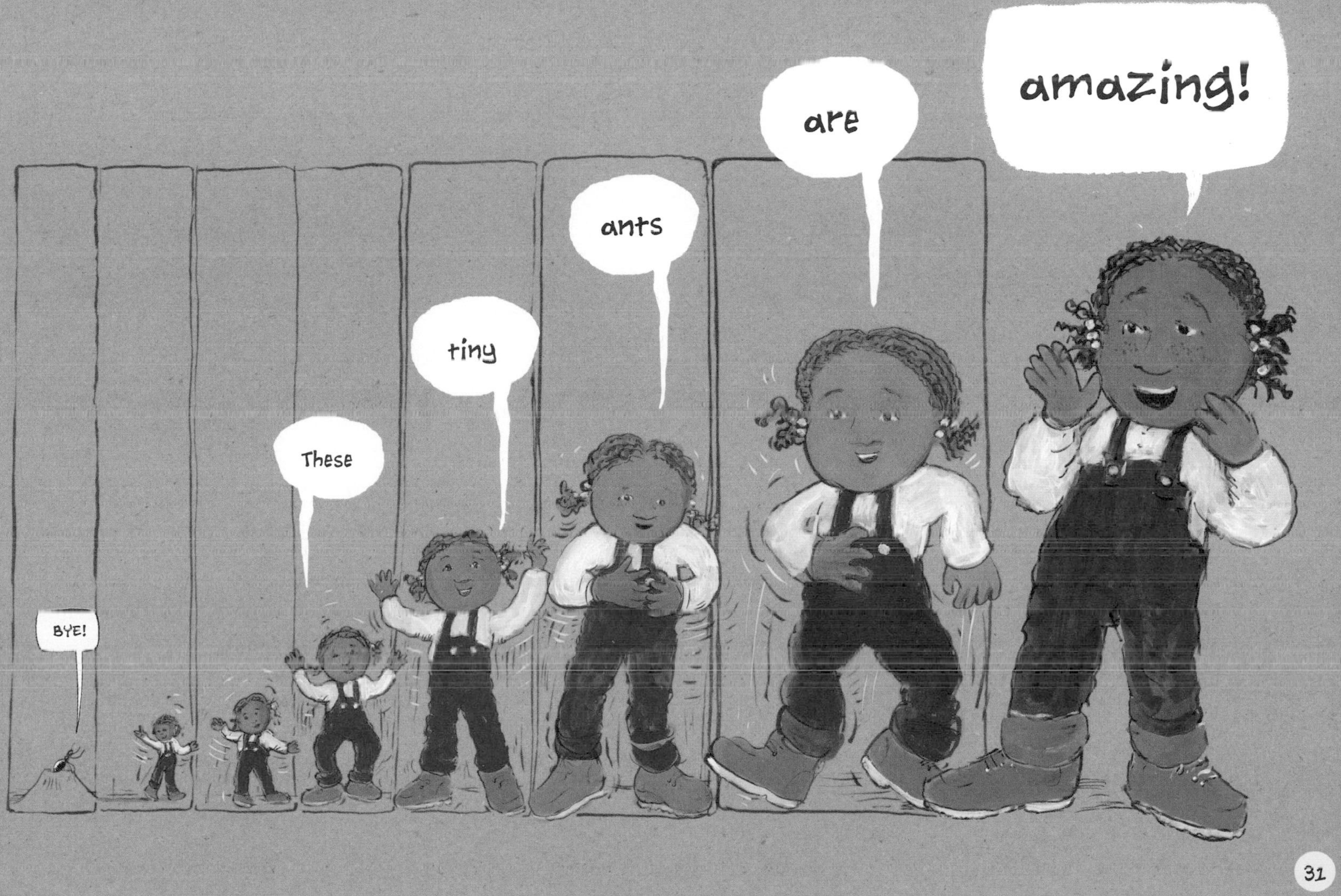
BYE!
These
tiny
ants
are
amazing!